Celebrating MOONSHINE music

Creativity, Culture & Cognizance

by *EyeNEye Goddess*
Inspired by the life & artistry of

B. Howard (Howard Soul)

Legends Never Fade. Their Legacies Live On.

Audience Advisory

This narrative contains strong language, adult themes, and mild sexual content. It is intended for readers 18 years of age and older. Reader discretion is advised.

First Edition
First Printing, 2026
ISBN: 979-8-218-48552-8
Library of Congress Control Number: 2025900283
Atlanta, Georgia
Cover design and illustrations by: Touqeer Shahid
Interior design and layout by: Sami Ahmed
Printed in the United States of America
For permission or inquiries, contact:
eyeam@eyeneyegoddess.org

Be soul-driven—create, share, inspire. Peace and positivity.

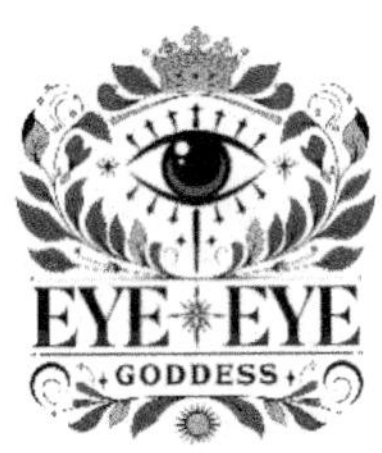

Disclaimer

This memoir intentionally uses slang and informal expressions to preserve authentic voice and artistic realism. These words reflect creative interpretation and the duality of B. Howard as expressed within the work.

Over five years, the lyrics in **Celebrating Moonshine Music: Creativity, Culture, & Cognizance** capture the essence of the artist's journey. Through dedication, audio interpretation, repeated listening, and reflective exploration, the material evolved to represent artistic perspective and expression. It stands as a creative tribute to the enduring voice and spirit conveyed within the work.

"That's a bet, that's a check, that's a 10-4, over. What up, blood? What up, cuz? What up, kinfolk?"

— B. Howard (Howard Soul)

The image that follows is a still from a video recorded by artist B.

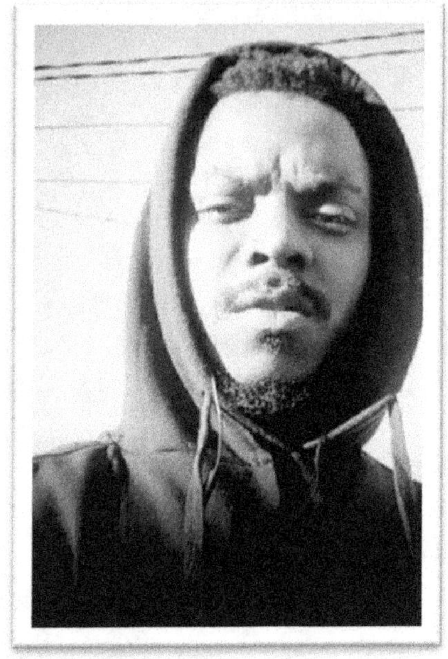 Howard (Howard Soul) On this day, he was outside, casually filming himself while rapping the hook to his song, "Dope." What started as a spontaneous moment became a powerful snapshot of his spirit: raw, and fully present. At first, I didn't think I'd use the clip. But when I watched it again, I felt the weight of it, carrying both strife and optimism; it spoke volumes, revealing how much truth and emotion lived in just that brief clip. Though B. Howard (Howard Soul) is no longer with us, this moment captured more than lyrics—it carried meaning. Preserving it here feels fitting, not just as a visual, but as part of his enduring legacy.

— EyenEye Goddess

Table of Contents

Book Synopsis

The Presence and the Past honors the life, voice, and work of B. Howard, also known as Howard Soul, through a tribute and continuation that preserves his creations as they were meant to be presented as a lyrical memoir. This work centers on three essential and inseparable forces: **Creativity, Culture, and Cognizance — the 3Cs.** Together, they shape art, literature, identity, and our understanding of the world, fostering connection, healing, awareness, and growth beyond the page.

Creativity is expression through spoken words, written text, melody, and movement. *Culture* is grounding in Southern roots, shared experiences, and collective histories that shape voice and meaning. *Cognizance* is awareness, a steady understanding of who we are, where we come from, and how our stories carry power. Through storytelling, truths are shared, wounds are acknowledged, and healing unfolds and uniqueness shines.

This lyrical memoir invites readers to embrace their own voices through art — building self-awareness, deepening community, and creating unity. As we build a collective circle of diverse identities, *creativity* becomes the bridge that transcends boundaries, uniting us through shared narratives across time and space. Storytelling carries the past into the present, shaping how we see the future.

In a community shaped by *creativity* and *culture*, *cognizance* grows. Shared expression becomes a source of strength, empowering us to reclaim and shape our narratives while bridging generations through the enduring power of voice. **Celebrating Moonshine Music: Creativity, Culture, & Cognizance** channels a musical force that resonates deeply, revealing the inseparable bond between music, memory, stories, and time.

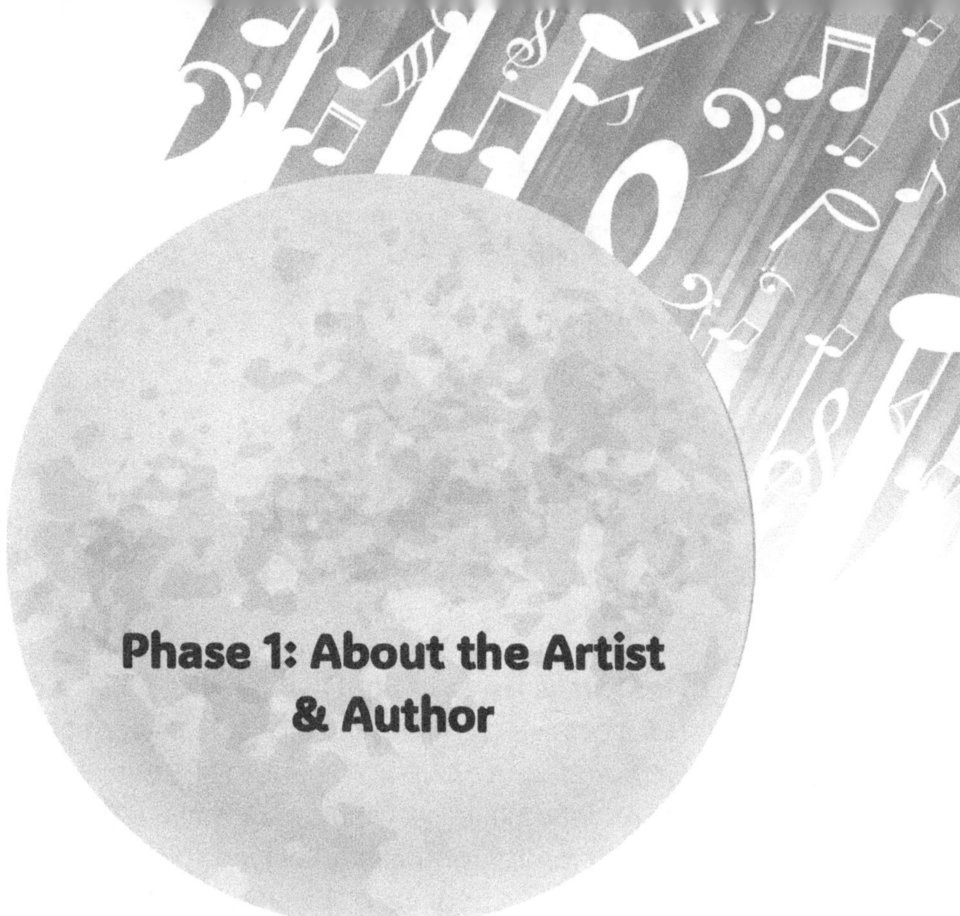# Phase 1: About the Artist & Author

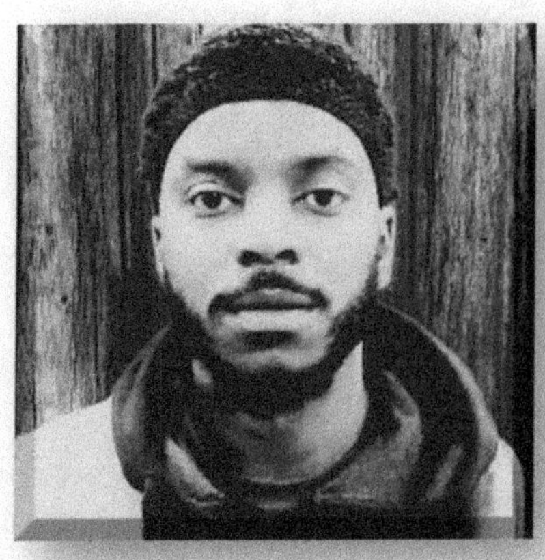

B. Howard also known as Howard Soul was a music artist known for his artistry and evocative recordings and private performances. He was from Georgia but grew up in the South Metro and the Southeast side of Atlanta. While growing up, B. Howard (Howard Soul) had a strong passion for football and played as a cornerback during his middle and high school years. Later in life, driven by his desire to master multiple trades, B. Howard (Howard Soul) obtained a forklift license and earned certification in Heating, Ventilation, and Air Conditioning (HVAC). He was skilled in multiple trades, including lighting and fixture installation, plumbing, drywall painting, and electrical repairs. He applied these abilities while traveling and working on various infrastructure projects. B. Howard (Howard Soul) later attended Georgia State University, where he was accepted into the highly competitive nursing program. During his time in the program, he worked as a Nurse Intern at Wellstar Health System and Grady Memorial Hospital. His exceptional ability to advocate for patients and ensure they received quality care earned him the nickname "Dr. Howard

Later on, B. Howard (Howard Soul) graduated from Georgia State University with an Associate of Applied Science in Nursing. He aimed to advance his nursing career by gaining clinical experience as a Registered Nurse (RN), becoming a Nurse Practitioner (NP), and eventually pursuing a scientific focus. In his leisure time he watched inspirational teachings and higher consciousness content while exploring his interest in science and chemistry. He also enjoyed watching football, movies, and special TV series. He loved trying new foods and visiting the latest restaurants, especially enjoying steak and shrimp.

He also had a special fondness for fresh fruit slushies. He loved working with his hands, fixing things, and teaching others, always eager to share his knowledge. He cherished passing on his wisdom to anyone willing to listen, traveling to discover unique places, and buying or collecting items he loved for himself and those close to him. As a mentor to many, he provided thoughtful advice, often analyzing situations by weighing the pros and cons. Not to mention fueled by a creative love for music, he expressed himself through rap, rhythm, and recording tracks that were raw, edgy, reflective, and fun, an embodiment of *creativity, culture, and cognizance.* Whether immersed in solitude, lost in the depths of his thoughts, or vibing with family and friends, the late-night hours became his sanctuary, a sacred time when life's complexities and inner thoughts transformed into resonant rhymes. This became a form of freedom, helping him release the weight of unspoken emotions.

As the caretaker of B. Howard (Howard Soul), I feel honored to preserve and share a glimpse of his past, ensuring his spirit and artistry continue to transcend time. Together, we had aimed to create a legacy through education, music, and community engagement, celebrating not only his artistic genius but also his deep commitment to offering second chances — a belief that every individual deserves a space where they feel respected, understood, and supported in their journey toward balance, purpose, and identity. My mission is to honor his memory through art and literature, weaving together *creativity*, *culture*, and *cognizance* in a timeless dialogue between the past, present, and future.

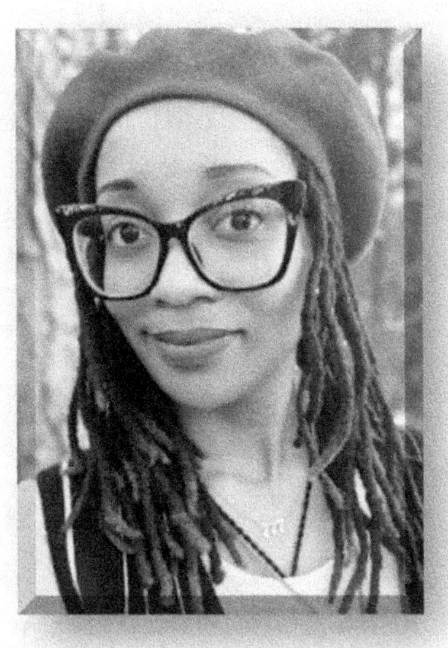

EyeNEye Goddess is a multifaceted educator, writer, and creative visionary from Georgia, raised in the Southeast. With this debut, she steps forward under the pen name EyeNEye Goddess, a creative identity that reflects the vision, insight, and expression she brings to her work. Her educational journey spans undergraduate and graduate studies in education, grounding her work in scholarship while honoring personal experience and cultural insight. She is a dedicated early childhood professional, researcher, and advocate committed to advancing early childhood and maternal-child health, strengthening community support systems and beyond.

EyeNEye Goddess brings expertise in early childhood education, providing specialized services for young children across public and private settings. Her work centers on collaborative, strengths-based approaches that nurture social, emotional, and cultural development, while honoring storytelling and diverse child-rearing practices. She implements interventions for young children and their families with a focus on overall health and well-being. At the heart of her work is a commitment to creating safe, supportive spaces where individuals can share their stories, learn, and grow. As a result of embracing diverse and cultural narratives, she believes an inclusive future can be achieved for the underrepresented. EyeNEye Goddess brings a transformative presence to education, weaving together insight, experience, and intention. Through her engagement with critical race theory and her educational journey, she developed a commitment to examining social structures and cultural identity, weaving *creativity, culture, and cognizance* into art and literature that amplify voice, visibility, and self-worth. EyeNEye Goddess finds joy in mindful adventures, painting, and sipping smoothies, while also indulging in travel and playful shopping sprees. Additionally, she enjoys exploring sound through music and pathways of transformation. She is dedicated to her educational growth and that of others. She successfully expresses her vision in this final line, which also connects to the larger themes of community transformation, education, and legacy.

Phase 2: Dedication

This lyrical memoir begins in gratitude, a song of thanks to the Most High God for making it possible to honor the life and legacy of B. Howard (Howard Soul) through these pages. Whether you knew him as B, Lil Brian, Young Beeta, B. Howard, Wild Wilborn, Shawty, Caveman, Howard Soul, Dr. Howard, or by another special name that holds a fond memory for you. As readers are invited into a personal journey where memories, emotions, reflections, and experiences intertwine, we welcome you to embark on a brief introspective experience — *Celebrating Moonshine Music* on our behalf. As you peruse these pages, bring along your imagination and or memory.

The goal is to collaboratively extend the narrative, creating a shared experience that resonates beyond the written word. *Creativity, culture, and cognizance* intertwine with the emotion of lyricism in this tribute to B. Howard, also known as Howard Soul. His words and lyrics continue to inspire and resonate across time. This work honors his legacy and *creativity*, bridging artistic expression and storytelling into a lasting tribute. As we embrace the 3Cs that encapsulate some of his emotions and emphasize the duality of B. Howard (Howard Soul)'s work, my perseverance has shaped his enduring legacy. In honor of him, I hope to connect with like-minded individuals and celebrate music and storytelling by capturing the essence of his spirit.

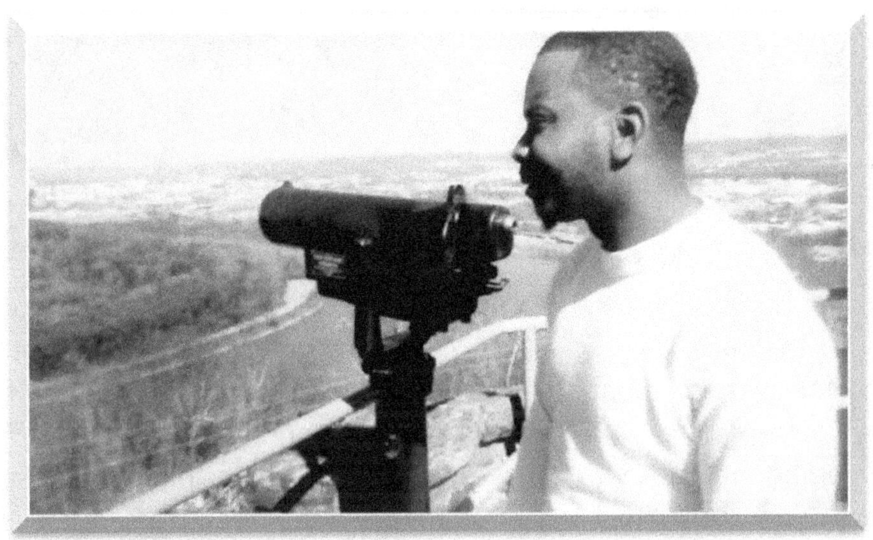

"I captured this moment in 2014: B. Howard standing on the
mountaintop, at peace, looking out across the scenery"

Phase 3: Acknowledgments

I come humbly before the Most High with a heart full of gratitude — for the Earth and Sky, for all living beings on land and in water, and for every element that makes up this world. I am thankful for the gift of life and committed to honoring my ancestors, remembering those who have passed, and cherishing all those I have connected with. I invite you to take a moment, close your eyes, and think of someone you miss who is no longer with us. Inhale the memory, and exhale gratitude for the gift of cherishing those moments and the meaningful connections they brought to your life.

Acknowledging your emotions is a crucial part of this journey. Whenever you feel ready, you should take a moment to express what is in your mind, throat, and heart. Memories are sacred holding truth we carry spoken or unspoken but always felt. Our ancestors' matter to us as much as we matter to them. Feel free to connect with them in whatever way feels meaningful. Join me in honoring the ancestors of B. Howard (Howard Soul) and me, both known and unknown, who continue to be a spiritual presence in our lives. We offer our deepest respect. We remember and honor those who came before us. To those whose legacy remains a guiding force—B. Howard (Howard Soul)'s beloved family members and our shared loved ones—I honor and cherish the lives of **Rathelia (Shawney); Pamela; Ethel Mae; Alfred; Melvin Sr.; Ida Mae; Willie Emma; Troy; Milton; Joe; and Sudie.**

While I hold their memories close to my heart, I am equally grateful for those who are still present with us today. I especially acknowledge the pillars of strength and light within the **B. Howard (Howard Soul) family—Ronald; Sarah; Catherine; and Angela.**

A heartfelt thank you goes to **Willie (Darryll) and Marquerite (Quita)** for their unwavering love and support that B. Howard (Howard Soul) throughout his life. I also honor **B. Howard (Howard Soul)'s siblings, nieces, nephews, godbrother's, godsister's, aunts, uncles, cousins, and dear friends.**

With deep appreciation, I extend love to my own immediate and extended family, especially **my mother** and **godmother**, as well as my **brother, sister, godbrother's and sister's, niece, nephews, godchildren, aunts, uncles, cousins. And friends** whose love and support carry me forward.

To all who continue to walk with us — B. Howard (Howard Soul), family and friends, and mine, your enduring love and presence enriches our lives and uplifts our spirits every day.

Peace and love to all. With gratitude for the hands, hearts, and minds that made this journey possible.

Phase 4: Preface

Everyone has a story worth sharing, and telling those stories is essential to preserving legacy beyond a lifetime. It becomes the responsibility of those who remain to celebrate and honor the memory of loved ones, showcasing their creations to the world through distinct language and expression.

This lyrical memoir reflects my desire to uphold the legacy and artistry of B. Howard, also known as Howard Soul, by capturing the emotions and messages woven into his music and lyrics. My connection to him extends beyond admiration. In personal moments, I remember Brian—the man behind the artistry. Yet within these pages, you will encounter B. Howard and Howard Soul, the creative forces whose names reflect distinct energies, emotional states, and unique lyrical wordplay.

Like B. Howard, he embodies a raw or anxious personality driven by inner tensions. This persona taps into the untamed side of *creativity*—through freestyle, narrative, or a lone verse—unleashing a bold, high-energy mood that carries an artistic intensity. Howard Soul embodies an introspective, observant persona, speaking from a place of relatability and emotional depth. His focus is on themes that reflect human experience and growth, whether in a single verse, verse-chorus structure, or spoken word. Together, these two identities create a dynamic musical experience. After he passed, I made the intentional choice to continue using the dual name to bring light to "Howard Soul"—a name he had begun to speak and embody during those late-night sessions. It became my way of preserving that evolution in his artistry.

Maintaining both names honors the fullness of who he was becoming and ensures that every layer of his creative identity is remembered. Their combined influence blends lively expression with thoughtful reflection, fostering growth, emotional resonance, and a unique reflection of *creativity, culture, and cognizance.*

As a result, I was motivated to create this project with passion and determination. Music has always been a powerful tool for connection, expression, and healing. For us, it played a significant role in the bond we shared. His passion for music, deep connections to various artists, and intimate conversations about life, love, and beyond are the foundation of this project. This short collection of memories and emotions led me to create this work to preserve his legacy and share the powerful impact that music and storytelling have on our lives. Brian once said, "Making music for the soul, I was born to do it." This simple yet profound statement captures his unwavering dedication to the craft. It was through music that we connected sharing sounds, emotions, and adventure.

Brian's love for music was infectious, teaching me that language and expression can connect us all. He drew inspiration from some of his favorite artists like André 3000, Big K.R.I.T., DMX, Kendrick

Lamar, and Nas—artists whose lyricism and storytelling shaped his perspective. Sometimes we bonded over the same artists; other times we explored different genres or remixes, discovering meaning in the contrast. No matter the lane, there was always that Southern undertone—something grounding and familiar. His energy and encouragement stayed with me; he would always say, "fuck it, do it," and remind me of one core truth: "forward progress, shawty," a call to keep moving.

Bob Marley was one of those bridges. His music embodied love and liberation—themes that resonated deeply with both of us. Songs like "Lively Up Yourself," "Natural Mystic," "Is This Love," and "Buffalo Soldier" became part of our shared soundtrack. We also gravitated toward songs that invited reflection. Tracy Chapman's "Fast Car" left a lasting impression with its storytelling and emotional honesty, prompting us to think about life's choices and the moments that shape who we become.

At times, we recognized our own story in the music we loved. Albums by Drake—*Thank Me Later* (2010), *Take Care* (2011), and *Nothing Was the Same* (2013)—felt like timestamps. Certain tracks seemed to mirror the emotional arcs we were experiencing, capturing feelings we sometimes struggled to articulate. Brian would joke that Drake was singing about things we had already lived through, as if the music understood us before we fully understood ourselves.

He also teased me about listening to Big K.R.I.T. "too much," though it was Brian who first introduced me to the artist by playing "Children of the World." From the opening beat to the lyrics and delivery, I was instantly drawn in. Big K.R.I.T. earned a permanent place on my list of favorites—alongside artists like Lil Wayne, whose early music introduced me to rap through rhythm, wordplay, and storytelling. My connection to music, though, started even earlier—in my youth. I remember being a little girl, riding in the truck with my dad, especially on Saturday mornings, when music would just play in the background. During those moments, I became fascinated with Tupac Shakur (2Pac) his presence, his voice, and the way his music felt. I recall even seeing him on TV, and hearing his songs play whenever I was around my dad. I may not have fully understood the depth of his words at the time, but something about his energy stayed with me. Even then, I was listening and absorbing in my own way.

Additionally, I'll give a shout-out to my brother, thanks to him, I became accustomed to every artist I was interested in. He made sure I had access to their music, buying me every album of every artist I liked, guiding my early journey, and shaping how I heard and felt music from the very beginning. Or, when I couldn't get a copy, I would just somehow find his CDs lying around and always find a way to listen to them—lol.

As I grew, somehow between my CD hunting and my brother's influence, I was drawn to the Southern sound of the late '90s and early 2000s. I first discovered the Hot Boys, including Lil Wayne, who were at their peak. Around the same time, I was also influenced by Pastor Troy, especially through *I Am D.S.G.B.*, rooted in Atlanta's Down South Georgia Boyz movement. Back then, I imagined myself as both DSGG—Down South Georgia Girl— shaped by the Southern influence I first felt when I heard "No Mo Play in GA" by Pastor Troy, and later connected to more deeply through "DSGB," and a "Hot Girl," inspired by "I Need a Hot Girl" by the Hot Boys—embracing that same bold confidence while staying rooted in my Southern identity as well.

That early connection stayed with me, and in time, it inspired me to create a lyrical memoir, guided by the artifacts left behind. I found inspiration in *The Rose That Grew from Concrete*, a book I had seen years ago by 2Pac but didn't read until the end of 2020. When I finally did, it resonated, affirming the power of expression, reflection, and storytelling through lyricism beyond time, and it gave me an idea spark to fulfill this project.

Continuing, I also found myself drawn to songs that carried deeper messages, which resonated with Brian. He appreciated Kendrick Lamar's storytelling and metaphor, especially tracks like "Swimming Pools (Drank)" and "Sing About Me, I'm Dying of Thirst." To us, Kendrick's music blended personal reflection with social awareness, connecting our own experiences to larger truths and ideas, and wordplay that illuminated both individual and collective experiences.

I was similarly introduced to the chemistry of artists like Starlito and Don Trip, whose collaborative projects demonstrated how two distinct voices could create something greater together. One memory remains vivid: Brian listening to a mixtape track titled "My Love." As I listened with him, the lyrics struck me — vulnerability and honesty woven into a reflection of relationships and responsibility. We often reminded each other to "tighten up," a phrase that acknowledged growth and accountability. The closing lines stayed with me: *I carry the world on both my shoulders and manage to still hold both her hands. She wants me to lift her up, but I need her to help me stand. Godspeed."* — Don Trip. Those words captured something we both understood — relationships require balance, and strength often comes from mutual support.

Adding to the memory, I still laugh thinking about the time Brian jokingly told me, "Bay, I think you used to be a singer for real." It wasn't a serious claim, just a playful observation about how open-minded I was with music. I played along with the joke, though only around him would I sing. I often sang R&B and favorites like Alicia Keys's "If I Ain't Got You" and Jazmine Sullivan's "Excuse Me." Brian enjoyed music too, especially Alicia Keys' "Diary." He would start a line, and I would finish it, turning small moments filled with shared energy. Looking back, I realize those moments revealed how deeply music shaped the way we connect and remain connected.

While I may not be a singer, I find purpose in writing—conveying messages, ideas, and emotions through words. I imagine possibilities across music commentary, reviews, storytelling, and cultural reflection. Writing allows me to bring ideas to life and make connections with others. Through my pen name, EyeNEye Goddess, I explore *creativity* and communication as tools for understanding and expression.

I am outgoing in speech and writing, yet it is through writing that I feel most deeply understood. The page becomes a space for clarity and emotional honesty. Words hold power, they shape perception and foster connection. Communication, when intentional, allows us to bridge experiences and ideas. Like Brian's passion for emceeing and public expression, I strive to use *creativity* and language as tools for meaning. My approach reflects the 3Cs: *creativity, culture,* and *cognizance,* for thoughtful expression and awareness.

Reflecting on *Bigger Than Life* by YG, with Nipsey Hussle and June Summers—a song B. Howard introduced me to, I'm reminded of his approach to music, grounded in purpose and presence. He was not driven by personal fame, but by a passion for creation and lasting impact. Much like the themes in the song, his music sought to transcend the moment and contribute something enduring—ideas and emotions that move others to express their own *creativity, culture, and cognizance.*

Though different in genre, *Use Somebody* by Kings of Leon—a song he loved, echoes a similar truth: where sound may shift, but the feeling stays the same, a feeling he held deeply. That feeling is carried through sound, memory, and connection.

Over time, I learned that music is more than entertainment; it is a vehicle for meaning and human connection. That understanding resonates with me. Whether through writing or reflection, I strive to contribute something meaningful—stories and ideas that encourage understanding and connection.

Brian and I shared a passion for education and music, recognizing their healing and transformative power. Writing and music allow emotional expression and foster connections rooted in shared memories and understanding. This belief awakens **The Celebration of Moonshine Music**—a fusion of **creativity, culture, and cognizance** that reflects the depth and purpose of this memoir and my vision of art and storytelling.

Phase 5: Introduction

How it started...

"Here, bay, keep this, cause you gon' need it one day."

— B. Howard (Howard Soul)

I was honored to share many moons with Brian—an intelligent and gentle soul whose quiet presence inspired those around him. I continue to hold his memory in high regard and am grateful for the moments we shared. His influence contributed to my personal growth and understanding of strength. Our connection reflected an evolution of life paths—an alignment of purpose that reached beyond mere love. It was a bond rooted in shared experiences and meaning, shaped by the belief that relationships can illuminate who we are and who we become.

We nourished each other and faced challenges together with resilience. I had fallen in love before I fully recognized it. It was something I always felt but could not fully understand. As we grew individually and together, it became clearer. I will always cherish your physical presence, emotional depth, spiritual insight, and everything else you gave me. I'm deeply grateful for all that you shared, and I often reflect on it. I honor your life by staying true to my word and continuing the vision you entrusted to me on this journey.

Brian, you will always be one of my greatest gifts, a bridge between the past and present. Living, learning, loving, growing, and creating cherished memories together was truly a pleasure. The time we spent together, embracing each other's love languages—and learning how to weave them all into our moments, from words of affirmation and quality time to physical touch, acts of service, receiving gifts, and even music was an irreplaceable gift.

I find peace knowing that your passion for teaching, sharing, and the arts of imagination and expression lives on through me—intertwined with your love, wisdom, and knowledge, and carried forward through my own passion, voice, and uniquely rooted purpose. Brian, as I move forward, I will continue to grow with everything you taught me, carrying all that we shared until your time in this realm came to an end. We were two spirits, destined to connect and uplift one another, evolving together while walking our separate paths, yet each on our own journey.

I will forever remember the joy you brought into my life. The times we thought would last forever may not, but they are eternal. The shared echoes of laughter, cries, smiles, disagreements, the fun, and the unpredictable moments will stay with me, transcending time and the afterlife. Together, we lived with purpose, sharing our truest selves. For every joy, lesson, and blessing — we gave, we grew, and I remain forever humble.

As I continue to grow and embrace my human journey, I carry the wisdom and insights from our shared moments. Your past encouragement continues to evoke me as I pursue the plans, dreams, and gifts ahead. The steps I take reflect your legacy and more as I move into the future. Brian, you were an unsung hero in my eyes, whose dedication to love and knowledge touched the lives of many.

You had an influence in the brief time you spent on this Earth with your family, friends, and especially me. Thank you for saving me. This lyrical memoir of B. Howard (Howard Soul)'s work, *Celebrating Moonshine Music,* is designed to encourage the *culture* of people to feel empowered to share their stories and truths as desired. I believe we all draw from shared experiences—love, loss, identity, healing, and growth—and that by embracing the full spectrum of our emotions, we can connect more deeply and share our craft. Creation comes to life when we speak, write, sing, or move, each vibration reaching us in both familiar and unfamiliar places. In this narrative, we present a musical force that strikes a distinct chord and resonates within the spirit. Our thoughts, dreams, and desires affirm that story and song are essential to the world. *Cognizance* unites *creativity* and *culture*, fostering connection rather than division. Claiming your narrative is power; awareness flourishes where *creativity* and *culture* meet. Words endure—they shape impact, preserve legacy, and light the path for others. To be heard begins with communication. Through speaking, writing, or music, these pages invite expression to unfold. Words may divide or unite, but through storytelling, we discover who we are, where we come from, and where we desire to go.

Driven by purpose and passion, stories build bonds that transcend barriers. ***Celebrating Moonshine Music: Creativity, Culture, & Cognizance*** preserves a legacy and shares musical treasures for generations to come. Storytelling offers me a path to healing for myself and others with similar experiences. Writing serves as a sanctuary and a place where thoughts are set free.

In my belief, words govern the universe; their interpretation shapes whether restoration brings healing or harm. I aspire to inspire not only those with musical gifts but communities everywhere, reminding us that freedom has no single path, and no story unfolds in a straight line. Each journey moves in its own rhythm, guiding us toward growth and purpose.

I seek to enrich others through affirmation and boundless conversation that encourages understanding, rooted in openness and free from shame. Storytelling and writing are powerful tools that shape minds from childhood through adulthood, nurturing awareness and connection. In this project, I center creative expression through music lyrics, embracing the truth that you are the author of your own story, whether grounded or imagination, as you move through life. My creative process flows through journaling, recording reflections, venting, writing notes to myself, and even sending texts, videos or emails to capture emerging ideas. These affirmations and insights become part of my ongoing evolution and expression.

Remember, boundaries are something we build every day in our own unique way, shaping how we engage with the world and protect our creative energy. Howard Soul once said, **"But time passes quite fast on its own. I'm all wrong, but I'm trying to get my shit right."** Remember to be optimistic in chaos or confusion. He said, **"You too can take a mental vacay."** I have faith that storytelling, writing, and music can foster healthy habits. Guided by a dedication to self-expression, I believe that releasing emotions through *creativity*—rather than suppressing them—can bring freedom, clarity, and peace to the mind.

Hold onto this truth — no one can tell or rewrite your story but you. Through challenges and triumphs, as B. Howard's logic, **"Maintain the forward progress within your one life to live."** Howard Soul said, **"And, so what I be tryna do is, I be wanting shit to ride, but I be tryna say some real shit, really rapping, but it be some more shit I be tryna teach at the same time, real shit."** In times of uncertainty, remember that you can express yourself by affirming your identity and what you stand for. This can be communicated through the 3Cs. Brian and I shared a passion for storytelling as a tool for empowerment—centering lives, shaping identities, and nurturing meaningful connections in pursuit of a liberated future. Howard Soul would often say, **"Build and born the youth,"** emphasizing how it shapes our lives today and, together, fosters identity and positive transformation for the future. **"Here, bay keep this, cause you gon' need it one day,"** is the essence of the connection to ***Celebrating Moonshine Music: Creativity, Culture & Cognizance,*** fueling a continuing legacy. It began with a compact disc (CD) labeled *'Moonshine,'* wrapped in notebook paper written with a black marker. Over time, I was entrusted with carrying the Moonshine spirit, sharing its music with the world, and awakening its mission through the artifacts he left behind.

You may be wondering, what exactly is *Moonshine Music*? It represents a journey that unfolds either after midnight or before sunrise. That magical moment when moonlight and music converge, crafting focus, and creative freedom with no limitations. Life often feels unclear, leaving us with surreal emotions that are hard to navigate. As a community, our shared experiences should remind us that healing comes through reflection, connection, detachment, and evolving truth I hold deeply as essential to growth. I believe a higher power has a greater plan for each of us, and that Earth is a temporary stop on our journey of growth and evolution.

Life brings us together, even briefly, in the shared pursuit of that growth. Legacies live on through the lasting memories we hold — like those of Brian's life and the musical gems he left behind. Brian, your legacy will continue to influence me as I navigate this transition with perseverance and purpose. You live in every life you touched. I carry you with me as a guiding spirit, not in absence. Our connection remains, honored and alive. I miss you deeply, and your legacy continues through my heart and the lives you inspired. I will honor your contributions by sharing one line at a time from *Moonshine Music*, letting your words echo and motivate educators, artists, writers, musicians, and beyond. As I continue this journey, I'll create, in the rhythm of life—because I know exactly where you are. And with every step, I will carry the movement forward, honoring *Moonshine Music* through *creativity, culture, and cognizance*—driven by both passion and purpose and rooted in legacy.

Fueled with fire and desire, I'll see you on the far side of the moon.

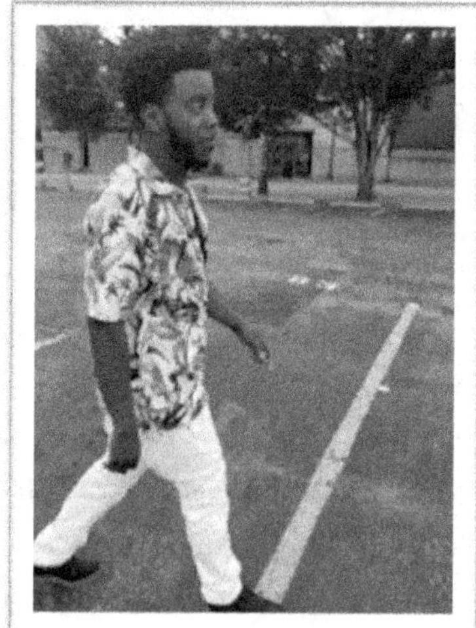

Eternal light and love
EyeNEye Goddess

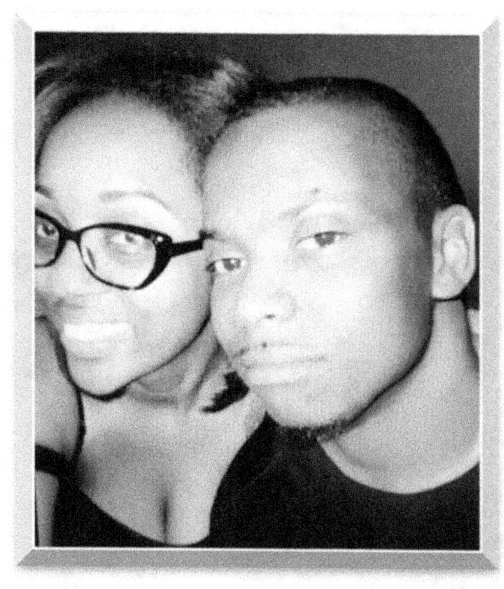

"One summer night, 2011/2012 — filled with laughter, love, and timeless memories"

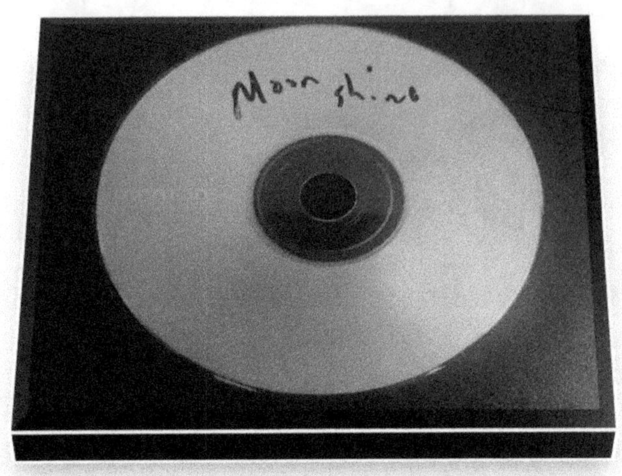

Artifact

This artifact is a compact disc (CD) titled *Moonshine*, originally wrapped in lined notebook paper with the word "Moonshine" handwritten boldly in black marker. The handwritten word on the CD reflects the nature of its creation. The CD was later placed into a standard CD case, preserving its origins —ready to shine.

B. Howard, B. Howard, B.
Howard-

B. Howard Dropping...

B. Howard, B. Howard, B
Howard-

B. Howard Rocking...

B. Howard, B. Howard B.
Howard-

B. Howard Popping...

B. Howard, B. Howard, B.
Howard-

it ain't no stopping...

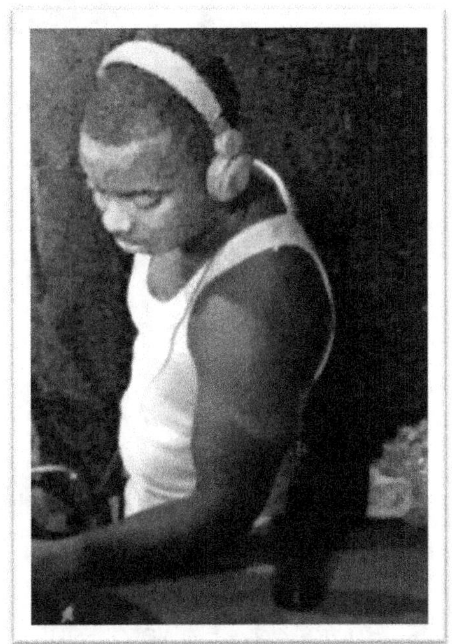

— B. Howard (Howard Soul)

"Brian in full B. Howard mode - peaceful, present, and lyrically
tuned. Rest easy, always in rhythm"

Song List

By: B. Howard (Howard Soul)

Moonshine Music

1. *DeStress (Get This Off My Chest)* – B. Howard
2. *My Flow* – B. Howard
3. *Dope* – B. Howard
4. *Never Fair (My G)* – B. Howard
5. *Inhale, Exhale* – Howard Soul
6. *The Oppressor* (Hate ur self)– Howard Soul
7. *P*N** – B. Howard
8. *Bout Geeked* – B. Howard
9. *Radioooo* – Howard Soul
10. *Lonely at the Top* – B. Howard
11. *Hallelujah* – B. Howard
12. *Wide Awake* – Howard Soul
13. *Mental vacation* – Howard Soul
14. *Survival of the Fittest (SOF)* – B. Howard
15. *What's the Point?* – B. Howard
16. *Bottom Out* – B. Howard
17. *Black Lives Matter (BLM)* – Howard Soul

Additional Songs

18. *Bobsleighed* – Howard Soul
19. *Blow* – Howard Soul
20. *Off-The-Cuff (Freestyle)* – B. Howard
21. *The News* – B. Howard
22. *Stick & move* – Howard Soul
23. *Cutthroat* – B. Howard

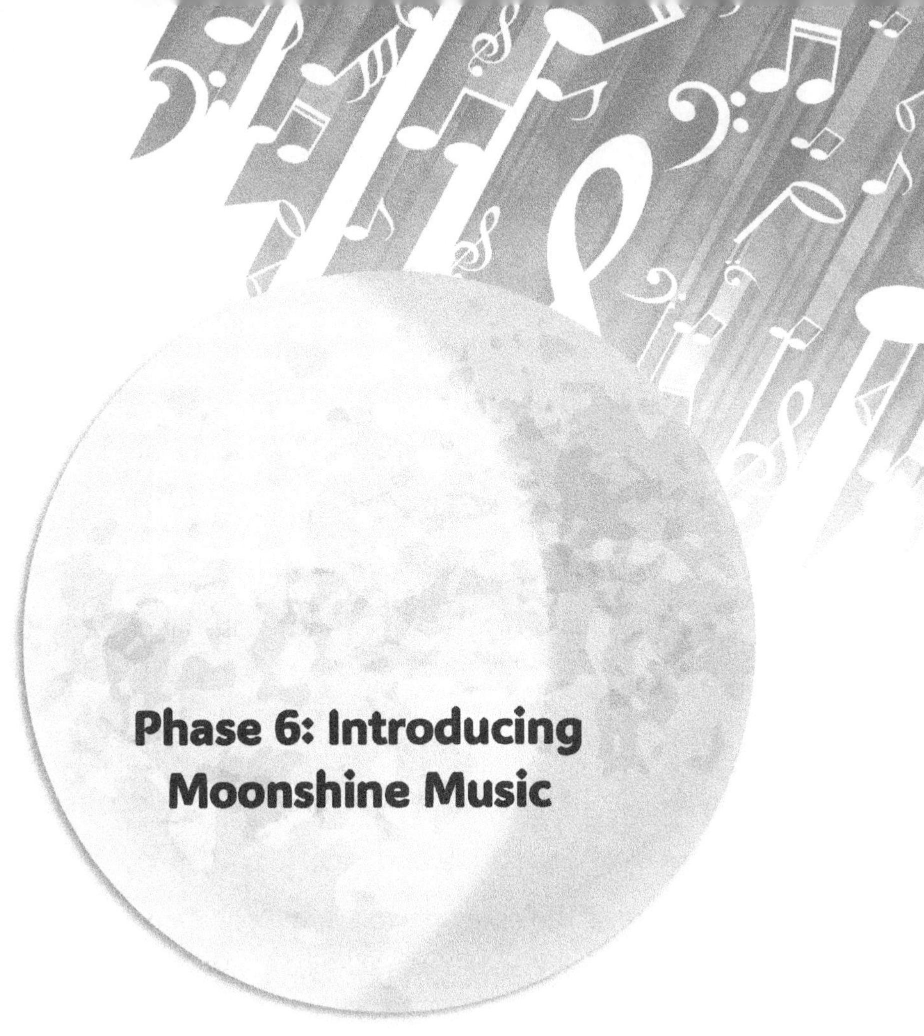

Phase 6: Introducing
Moonshine Music

DeStress

(Get This Off My Chest)

[Chorus]

Get this off my chest, going through some stress,

Gotta get this off my chest- get this off my chest,

Going through some stress,

Gotta get this off my chest- get this off my chest.

[Verse 1]

If only God could judge me what the fuck is Judge for,

They caught my Unk with dope and gave 'em 10 at the front door,

Oh, I guess they playin' God. I think like a jihad.

See everybody wanna part but won't play they part.

And everybody wanna start, but don't practice hard.

I put my heart in this hard, man, I swear to God.

Ain't gettin' paid for no shows, ain't got no groupie hoes,

Ain't got no purple-label clothes or no 24s.

I'm just preachin' what I know, tryin' save souls.

And in return, they curse my name, and throw low blows,

But look me in the eye, and see I ain't afraid of death,

The last of the Mohicans, I'm the last real nigga left.

[Pre-Chorus]

I cook, I chef, but I ain't talkin' bout no cocaine.

My music be good for your head like Rogaine propane. I'm no game,

I shine, need no chain. Planner my domain, sent here to shake shit.

Caveman my nickname, I live life so basic.

[Verse 2]

Life's a bitch, face it, hugged the hoe, embrace it,

See, I kissed my mama, cold body. Told her rest in peace,

And I won't let nobody. Come between me and my sista, I mean, nobody.

Before that, I put holes through they whole body.

Ain't lying, Amen then I shut the casket now I walk without a heart because

my mama has it.

It's in the ground, I ain't playin' around Ion even need a hook,

I can see through them like glass and read these niggas like a book,

These niggas shook, and they should be, 'cause I don't gotta flex and rap

For folks to feel me, You feel me?

[Bridge]

See, they brought us here on slave boats gave our ass a language,

Now we get to eat with 'em,

Thinkin' that's gon' change shit but watch them folks get 'hind yo ass,

See if they gon' change shit.

The goal is to lock our mind or lock us in containment.

[Verse 3]

So, Ima paint the white house Black, Ima sell white folk crack

Turn this world on its back

Cause I don't know how to act

Woke up this mornin' with a hard dick.

Like fuck the world, I'm bout to start shit

No rubber on, rest in peace, my momma gone,

But I'm *Whining (Wine 'ing)* no Sutter Homes

Soldier must keep movin' on Haha, Ima do that

I was told we was Jews really can they do that,

They lie about history, now Ion know what's fact, in fact bout to get this off my chest,

[Outro – Faded Talking]

You know what I'm saying, some shit like that, boi, just like that, that shit perfect.

My Flow

[Chorus]

Runnin' through these hoes like a red light, red-light,

Bitch said I was drunk, she was dead right, dead-right,

Enlight Ent, gon' get that head right, head-right,

Put that ass to sleep, don't let the bed bugs bite — ouch,

[Verse]

Baby momma, put you out, but homes, I won't laugh at that

I could steal a nigga flow, but I am not a piggyback

Tick for tack, pound for pound, overall and all around,

Howard got that unique sound, it's coming in the underground,

Hip-hop, thrift-shop, slow niggas can't compete,

Passed out a thousand CDs and they still in the street.

Getting rained and pissed on, it's okay, just stay strong

I might let ya piggyback if yo ass can hang on.

[Chorus/Outro]

Can you hang on? **(Repeat 3x)**

If your ass can hang on. **(Repeat 3x)**

Margins of My Mind

(Connected to lyrics on next page)

"Dope" carries a nostalgic energy that resonates with *culture* and individual experience. It blends struggle, survival, and community insight — reflecting life as a Black male in the inner city. B. Howard bridges survival with cultural roots, revealing a layered brilliance in both intellect and sound. To me, these lyrics reflect his growth, resilience, and depth.

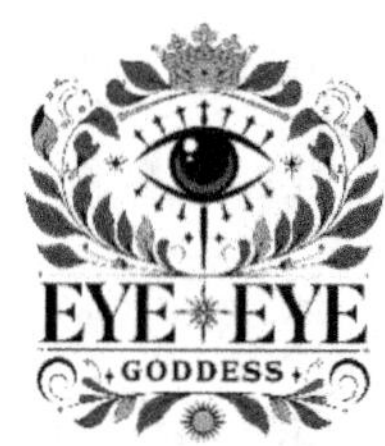

Dope

[Intro]

I'm ready, don't nobody wanna play no real shit no mo, man.

Shit, they always want that crunk shit.

[Chorus]

Wish they played the real shit as much as they play crunk shit
(Repeat 5x).

[Verse 1]

I wish they played the real shit as much as they play crunk shit,

Maybe we'll act mo civilized instead of monkey.

Maybe it wouldn't be no dope boys cause it's no junkies.

Nigga, keep dreamin' and keep that trap bonkin'.

[Hook]
(Repeat 2x)

Right away Dope.

Dope. **(Repeat 3x)**

Right away

[Verse 2]

Now everybody wanna be a trapper, make a sale, nigga.

But before you get that key, you probably get a cell, nigga.

And life is what you make it — why you make it hell, nigga?

Say you wanna make a difference, shit, I can't tell, nigga.

Real shit, the afterlife ain't promising ahhun,

So I hope you find somethin' you know mo' than money

On this planet, goddammit, why do I try? I try.

When bad bitches only thang they like, only thang they like: Good gas to smoke — huh, don't laugh, it ain't no joke.

Nigga cool as hell till you dumb as hell, standing up in court.

Put out the pote, let me get some fresh air.

They say, "Better days comin'," I just hope I'm still here to see 'em .

[Bridge]

They say they charging two limbs — that's a arm and a leg,

Or a spy in the Fed. They say, "Howard, you scared?"

Nah, I been there, done that, and I bet nine out of ten,

Ya mama ain't smoke crack.

[Verse 3]

Come here, come here.

Aye, me and Grandpa watched *In the Heat of the Night.*

Ain't seen my mama in two weeks, she in the heat of the night.

Uncle Q came through when he sold out of white.

I think he felt sorry for me — he would buy me them Nikes.

Neighborhood full of junkies, they were higher than kites.

You know the story: Smart king with a troublesome life.

Uncle Gary said, "Brian, you better learn how to fight,

Or sell some wolf tickets." I was lacking the height.

It was Cleveland, for Bleveland', Stewart for Metro.

If you wanted you some pussy, you could buy you a hoe.

Club Nikki, Magic City, where the ballers would go.

And old Bobby ran numbers before we had a lotto.

[Outro]

Starter jacket started hella shit — hella shit.

Nigga would get they ass kicked for the hell of it.

Snort a bit, sell a bit, now that's irrelevant.

Enough about me, I'm just telling you how it was growing up in the
3, fuckin' wit —

[Chorus/Outro]

Dope **(Repeat 4x).**

Wish they played the real shit as much as they play crunk shit.

Dope **(Repeat 2x).**

Wish they played the real shit as much as they play crunk shit.

Dope **(Repeat 4x).**

Wish they played the real shit as much as they play crunk shit.

Maybe we'll act mo civilized instead of monkey.

My Heart Between His Lines
(Connected to lyrics on next page)

Among many, "Inhale-Exhale" is a favorite — the acoustic vibe moves my soul with every beat. I find the hook resonates with me when practicing breathwork. Relaxing into a meditative state, inhale and be still, exhale and be present, remember and be thankful for your presence on this planet. I feel this work celebrates the art of storytelling, where street knowledge illuminates the path and ghetto wisdom echoes in the hearts of listeners. Move at your own — pace, the journey is yours to shape.

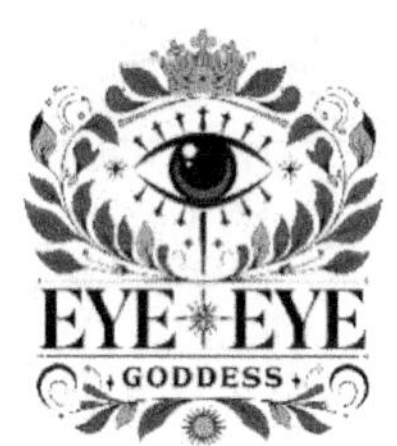

Inhale-Exhale

[Hook]

Inhale, Exhale, Inhale, Exhale — Breathe. **(Repeat 4x)**

[Verse 1]

Only God knows why He put me on this Earth.

Ten toes, ten fingers — bless the healthy birth.

Learned about the world and how some things work,

But I just wanna ride Binz before I ride a hearse.

Wasted a lot of time chasing dope boy dreams,

Tryna fuck hoes, tip-toe a triple beam.

Atlanta, '80s baby — you was born into it.

But making music for the soul, I was born to do it.

My friends say I changed 'cause I am tryna win.

Dropped out the first time, now I'm back again.

Working full-time, and I'm turning papers in.

If they say I'm lame, then I don't need a friend.

I got a girl, I got a girl, and she down as hell.

Found a number in my cell, now she raising hell.

Ima stay little Brian, you know, chasing tail,

But I lose every girl I love tryna be a playa.

And for your information, there were houses on new plantations.

The slave owner signs off the checks and vacations.

This just a demonstration of a false emancipation,

'Cause freedom can't be given — freedom must be taken.

Think about it — before I bought it, did I really need it?

Or did I just get it for the hoes to see it?

Even worse, did I do this shit for the niggas?

Threw on my Js and my yays like Ima kill these niggas, damn.

[Hook]

Inhale, Exhale, Inhale, Exhale — Breathe. **(Repeat 4x)**

[Verse 2]

So let me ask you, how hard do you want it?

No cut for my opponent, straight raw — you still want it?

Not really, thought I was selling, not really.

I need dilly, no love, I ain't from Philly, ah!

Nope, I ain't from Philly, ah!

ATL, Georgia, nigga, home of the peach drop,

Where they used to hang Black folks like sheetrock.

Junky by blood — I was raised in the mud.

Keep a rifle close by like a young Elmer Fudd.

And my vices and habit keep me filling this tablet

With a lot of real shit, so all my people can have it.

Is you got 'em, or savage? Regular, average?

Them boys give a damn if you got loud or babby.

They still run in yo' shit for a gravy lick,

Go spend half on a fit, then half on a bitch — hah!

Kind of funny, sad at the same time.

You don't gotta have yours, but I gotta have mine, soooo…

[Hook]

Inhale, Exhale, Inhale, Exhale — Breathe. **(Repeat 4x)**

[Verse 3]

A damn shame — if you don't bang, you a soft nigga.

But ain't no blood or no crip done help me out, nigga.

Probably done shop with me, probably done sold me something,

But when I first got out, they couldn't loan me nun'.

To each its own, them niggas grown, and I ain't big on judging.

I just threw that shit out there for my little cousin,

Tryna save him so my aunt and unc don't have to grave him.

Before them —

Shit, they killed Mike, left his brains on the step.

I couldn't fly to California, but many nights I wept.

So, if you ever have to kill a brotha,

I hope it's before a reason other than a color.

Bang, bang — I lost my mother in these same streets.

Every time I pop a pill, pray I don't OD.

Know it's sad, but it's truth, 'cause that's all I kicks:

Ghetto knowledge minus all the politics.

[Hook]

Inhale, Exhale, Inhale, Exhale — Breathe. **(Repeat 4x)**

Never fair

(My G)

[Intro]

It's just how I feel,

How I feeeeeel,

How I feel, how I feel,

Just how I feel, how I feel.

[Hook]

Life is never fair to you, life is never fair to me,

And your least catastrophe: tragedies and casualty.

Robberies and suffering call the land of broken dreams,

Hear them little babies scream, nothing never what it seems.

[Verse]

I got nieces, I got nephews — I can't buy nobody shit.

How you think that make me feel? Boy, that make me feel like shit.

I be riding with my tool, I be thinking 'bout a lick.

I be filling out these apps — they ain't calling back for shit.

They tryna take they car.

WTF I get this note for? Sleeping on the sofa.

I hope this drought bout over,

'Cause I can't take no mo', bro.

At least with God, I'm closer.

Going through a lot, I need a break like Rotor.

Guess poverty just a part of me, like an artery.

Why shit gotta be so hard for me?

I don't wanna hit no robbery or no jack moves.

If I have to, you got me and my choppa be in yo' spot,

Pulling straight up out yo' pocket — in the bank would be too hot.

As I ponder and I wonder:

How I da get outta here, my G?

While you right here with me, won't you put one in the air wit me?

I ponder and I wonder:

How I da get outta here, my G?

While you right here with me, won't you put one in the air wit me?

[Hook]

Life is never fair to you, life is never fair to me,

And your least catastrophe: tragedies and casualty.

Robberies and suffering call the land of broken dreams,

Hear them little babies scream, nothing never what it seem.

Margins of My Mind

(Connected to lyrics on next page)

To me, this mirrors the struggles and experiences of oppressed people. A mirror held up to those who've been disconnected from their roots. For some, having a sense of identity is a constant struggle, especially when *culture* has been stripped away or distorted. When there's no clear direction, no sense of belonging or connection to something greater, it's easy to feel lost. Internalized racism and societal conditioning are powerful forces that teach people to devalue themselves and their heritage.

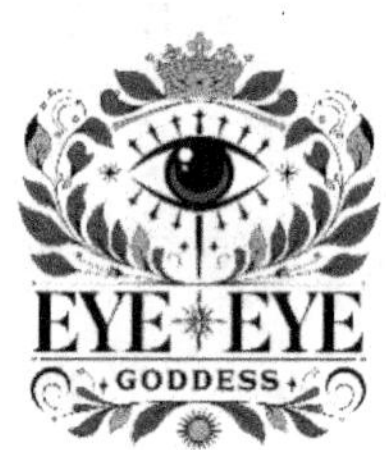

The Oppressor
(Hate ur self)

Inspired by Malcolm X's enduring question posed powerfully in his 1962 speech — "Who taught you to hate yourself?"

[Verse]

Feeling stranded since we landed on foreign turf,

Don't need no man to get to God, so I don't go to church.

It ain't no luck, and it's all fate, so you gon' get this work,

And when that monkey on yo' back, you can't fit yo shirt.

This shit berserk, but Ion give a fuck.

And some waiting on the Mothership to pick 'em up.

Pick up my cup, pick up my blunt — that's my pick-me-up.

My shit hard, and it's coming — put the pussies up.

Punch line, punch line, but that don't mean shit.

That's all them other rappers spit 'cause they ain't seen shit.

Either that, or they don't know shit,

A downfall of having ignorant associates.

Tighten up that circle — they gon' murk you 'fore they help you out.

Make the most out of yo' life before you exit out.

I been about telling niggas they should stick together,

One for all, all for one, defeat the oppressor (echo).

Pussy Nigga

[Intro]

Yeah, yeah, yeah, yeah,

Hell you talkin' 'bout?

Yeah, yeah Ion know.

[Hook]

(Repeat 1X)

Now he lay me down to sleep, yeah,

Pray the Lord my soul to keep, yeah, yeah.

Keep that thang, these niggas creep, yeah, yeah,

7 days, these niggas weep

[Hook]

(Repeat 2x)

Now he lay me down to sleep, (Now he lay me down to sleep)

Pray the Lord my soul to keep, (Pray the Lord my soul to keep)

Keep that thang, these niggas creep, (Keep that thang, these niggas creep

7 days, these niggas weep (7 days, these niggas weep) — pussy nigga.

[Verse]

In the crowd, you loud — so low, you so low.

I can't hear you, bitch nigga, huh, take a shot of liquor.

Mister, get some hair on ya chest. If you wasn't so flaw,

You'd be rocking with us.

Extended family in the bitch — it's about a thousand of us.

Now you're out your ailment, and you don't know how to adjust.

Yeah, we drankin' and we smokin' while the Bible with us,

But we ain't claim to be no saint, so don't you start that fuss.

Yeah, he flippin' and he trippin' 'cause he on that dust.

Give a damn about your high — you better not trip on us.

Look, I'm jumpin' off the deep end for no apparent reason.

It's duck-hunting season — I hear a lot of quackin'.

They doin' this, they doin' that, they doin' a lot of actin'.

I'm strategically attackin' all these sucka niggas rappin', *porque, porque.*

My people stay in no fucked-up position,

And it's been proven: if you talk, somebody gotta listen.

[Hook]

(Repeat 2x)

Now he lay me down to sleep, (Now he lay me down to sleep)

Pray the Lord my soul to keep, (Pray the Lord my soul to keep)

Keep that thang, these niggas creep, (Keep that thang, these niggas creep

7 days, these niggas weep (7 days, these niggas weep) — pussy nigga.

Bout Geeked

[Intro]

Lil Playa from the Soufside,

Ya feel me?

It's some real shit now.

[Hook]

(Repeat 2x)

Popped two perks, 'bout geeked.

'Bout geeked. **(Repeat 5X)**

Riding on 285, 'bout sleep.

'Bout sleep. **(Repeat 5X)**

Fuck it, me and my shit on repeat.

On repeat. **(Repeat 5X)**

Kick my bitch out.

She out. **(Repeat 5X)**

Pistol to the seat.

Her seat. **(Repeat 4X)**

[Verse]

I want head and tails, bottom and top,

Wanna stick it in the yaya till I make them leg lock.

Fred Flintstone bedrock, x got her shell shock,

Left a little message for her, stuck it in her mailbox.

Hurry, hurry, urgent, urgent,

I be workin' it for certain,

Pop that pussy till she squirtin',

Pop that pussy till she squirtin'.

Splash, splash, that's my shit,

Hashtag at yo bitch,

Here's my number and my kick, I'm just playing, kicking shit.

She don't like short niggas, I don't like broke bitches,

We both SOL, might as well switch them digits.

Might as well let me hit it, I won't tell yo' secret, I don't kiss and tell,

I won't be no witness.

Yeah, I promise, yeah, I promise, I won't tell a damn soul,

But if y'on play yo' role, you can gon' hit the road.

Yeah, I promise, yeah, I promise, I won't tell a damn soul,

But if y'on play yo role,

You can hit the road.

[Hook]

(Repeat 2x)

Popped two perks, 'bout geeked.

'Bout geeked. **(Repeat 5X)**

Riding on 285, 'bout sleep.

'Bout sleep. **(Repeat 5X)**

Fuck it, me and my shit on repeat.

On repeat. **(Repeat 5X)**

Kick my bitch out.

She out. **(Repeat 5X)**

Pistol to the seat.

Her seat. **(Repeat 4X)**

Eternal Resonance

(Connected to lyrics on next page)

From the beginning, "Radioooo" was a unique song with a chill flow. The intention of the song, at least through my lens, is Howard Soul's confidence and persistence in rejecting mainstream music in favor of something personal and unique to you. Find your own sound and voice. Creating music that feels authentic helps you stay grounded. Rock in your own zone — stand out by walking to your own beat. Sometimes, you have to go against the mainstream to be heard. Do what resonates with you — if you're speaking, someone will listen. So be you, be true!

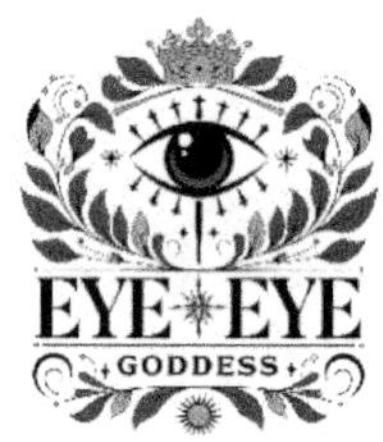

Radioooo

[Intro]

Ion like it.

I don't.

Fuck it.

[Hook]

(Repeat 2X)

Ion like the radio. Shit made my own song. *(radioooo)*

I be rockin' rockin' (Rockin') (Rockin') (Rockin') in my own zone.

I be rockin' rockin' (Rockin') (Rockin') (Rockin') in my own spot.

And I stay rockin' rockin' (Rockin') (Rockin') (Rockin') 'til I'm on top.

[Verse 1]

If Cupid was real, tell the midget to shoot me.

Cause usually my heart cold, covered up by fake smiles.

Ask me, I'm God's child,

Technically Jesus' brother.

Yeah, I said it, didn't stutter.

Amped up in this motherfucker.

Stunned all the shit I spit; people say my mind sick.

Naw, I'm just sick of it, and them people full of shit.

Feces, a pile of it. When you real, the crowd loves it.

Haters gon' hate. When you focus, you just fly above it.

[Hook]

(Repeat 2X)

Ion like the radio. Shit made my own song. *(radioooo)*

I be rockin' rockin' (Rockin') (Rockin') (Rockin') in my own zone.

I be rockin' rockin' (Rockin') (Rockin') (Rockin') in my own spot.

And I stay rockin' rockin' (Rockin') (Rockin') (Rockin') 'til I'm on top.

[Verse 2]

I was just fast-food working, tech school attending.

Nigga from the bottom tryna to see a happy ending.

But they didn't want to listen without no true religion.

If you ain't got no Bugatti or you ain't shooting nobody,

They should sit on the potty with my little cousin Dre.

Cause I swear they all-all full of bullshit anyway.

I'm still in debt, no Icy chain yet.

Just these old shoe strings, and keys round my neck.

But you don't know success by material things.

How many cars you drive, or no pinky ring.

So, what's the new day bring? For a nigga, down and out.

My problem's I'm drowning out.

With weed and liquor,

I'm fucked up.

[Hook]

(Repeat 2X)

Ion like the radio. Shit made my own song. *(radioooo)*

I be rockin' rockin' (Rockin') (Rockin') (Rockin') in my own zone.

I be rockin' rockin' (Rockin') (Rockin') (Rockin') in my own spot. And

I stay rockin' rockin' (Rockin') (Rockin') (Rockin') 'til I'm on top.

My Heart Between His Lines

(Connected to lyrics on next page)

Life is a journey of discovery, and love — though imperfect — is something we come to understand through experience. What may appear as illusions often transform into reality if we resist accepting life's natural course. Embracing both the highs and lows with an open heart deepens real understanding and strengthens resilience in self. This song captured a difficult time in our relationship — it was during that season of struggle the song was created. You can hear the truth, and the vulnerability woven through the lyric. Yet, in success, be cautious, as it's often lonely at the top. What glitters is not always gold. Staying grounded in humility and openness will guide you through the obstacles.

Don't lose sight of connection during chaos or confusion. Distractions can alter your path. Be patient, stay persistent — and most importantly, don't fold because the grass is not always greener on the other side.

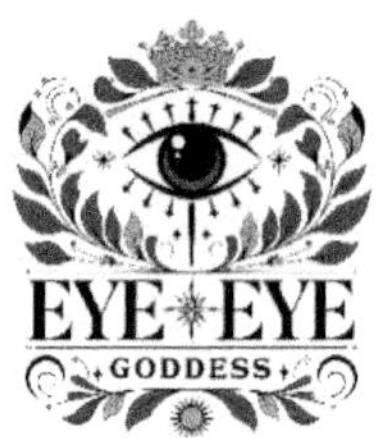

Lonely At the Top

[Intro]

They say, **(Repeat 8x)** (Faded)

It's Lonely at the Top

They say, **(Repeat 5X)**

[Hook]

(Repeat 2X)

They say it's lonelyyyyyyyy at the top (at the top)

But it's lonely at the bottom too,

I don't know what Ima do without you(echo)

Guess, I'm just gon' have to do without you(echo)

[Verse]

Friends a flip on ya, girl a dip on ya,

Scared to get hurt so, I just stay a loner.

Tryin' get my life together,

And in the process, I can't worry about another fella.

Rich and fame ain't everything sound cliché,

But money can't buy happiness and that's a guarantee.

People come, people go, in and out ya life,

Born alone, die alone, that don't have a price.

Many nights, It's me and my pad,

Thinking bout the past, love one's past,

How long does love last?

Cause I'm lost.

And if you were a boss, could you really pay the cost?

And have the heart to cut some real loyal people off?

Conversation, rule the nation, I can go for that,

But once you've burned too many bridges, you can't travel back.

They say it's lonely at the top, I didn't tell you that,

But if I ever make it there, I'll let you know the fact.

[Hook]

(Repeat 2X)

They say it's lonelyyyyyyyy at the top (at the top)

But it's lonely at the bottom too

I don't know what Uma do without you(echo)

Guess, I'm just gon' have to do without you(echo)

Eternal Resonance

(Connected to lyrics on next page)

I can still recall the instrumental playing over and over in 2011, weeks before the lyrics were added. Whether we were together in the house, driving, or just talking on the phone, the beat was always playing somewhere nearby. Such a nostalgic memory. There was a time when we delved deeply into the nuances of religion and beyond, discussing the significance of history, its representation, and how it intertwines with personal spirituality. "Hallelujah" became a shared expression during those times, capturing reflection and personal realization.

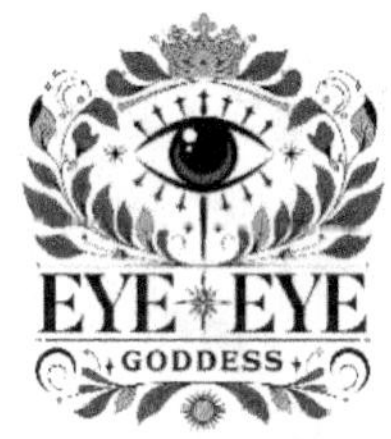

Hallelujah

[Hook]

Hallelujah, hallelujah, hallelujah, hallelujah, ha-ha-ha-hallelujah, hit!

Hallelujah, hallelujah, hallelujah, hallelujah, ha-ha-ha-hallelujah, hit!
Hallelujah, he ain't talkin' bout the future, so tired of futuristic swag,

I'm tired of the future. Already, my soldiers ready, already, like Armand Getty

Is around the fuckin' corner, and around the fuckin' corner,

It's some niggas who don't wanna, listen to the truth, either they scared or just don't wanna.

Hear it cause they fear it, fear it cause it hurts, and that real really hurts, so they don't get this deep in church, hit!

[Hook]

(Repeat 4X)

Hallelujah, hallelujah, hallelujah, hallelujah, ha-ha-ha-hallelujah, hit!

[Verse]

Hallelujah, thank God for settin' me free,

I don't wanna fit in, no mo, I'm doin' me.

Aye, let's show unity, or agree to disagree, how bout we learn our history, before we end up history.

Hallelujah, I got a mind of my own, and I don't feel bad 'bout smoking' on strong.

On the microphone, you will not hear me stutter, cause I do not feel bad by droppin' knowledge on my brothers.

They should pay me like the others, but they say I will not sell,

Cause I'm straight to the point, and I raise a lot of hell.

And I shall, and I shall reign bells, hell yeah,

And I shall, and I shall reign bells, but Ian King, hit!

[Hook]

(Repeat 4X)

Hallelujah, hallelujah, hallelujah, hallelujah, ha-ha-ha-hallelujah, hit!

[Outro – Faded Talking]

[Hook]

Hit!

(Repeat 4X)

Hallelujah, hallelujah, hallelujah, hallelujah, ha-ha-ha-hallelujah, hit!

Hit, Hit (echo)

Hit!

Hallelujah

Hit, Hit (echo)

Margins of My Mind

(Connected to lyrics on next page)

There is a smooth and assertive melody to this track that I find extremely admirable. To me, the flow shows Howard Soul's confidence — his ability to beat the odds using sharp, catchy wordplay that defines him as an artist and more. Speaking the honest truth is what you get in this short masterpiece.

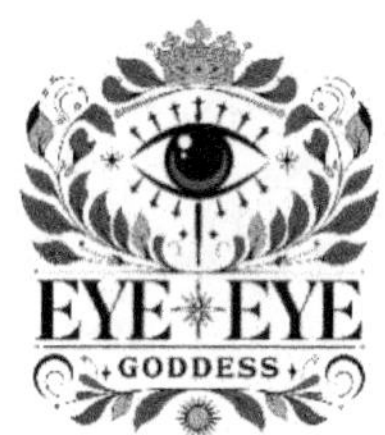

Wide Awake

[Intro]

No, no, no, noooooooooooooooo

[Hook]

(Repeat 2X)

No break no sleep

No break no sleep

No break no sleep

No break no sleep -No, no, no, noooooooooooooooo

[Bridge]

Yeah, no surrender no retreat, I will never quit,

'Til they put that fluid in me and that death certificate.

No, no, no, noooooooooooooooo

[Verse1]

Watch me kill it for it start that's abortion.

Getting mine off top, that's extortion.

If you find my rap book, that'll be a fortune.

But ion write shit, might as well keep recording.

That'll be good for ya maybe they'll do it for ya

Or quit rapping altogether find a new employer

Heard ya do a lot of talking, try a news reporter

And since you like the law so much, go and be a lawyer,

Cause I do this, no matter what my mood is

I just beat the honest truth, and I make you boys look foolish.

Without no pen or practice, my flow on point like cactus

I'm the best around the globe; nigga go pick up an atlas

Laid your girl on the mattress Como Telle Vu

Now I heard you want to fight me, watch me beat that ass like
Roots,

Heard you wanna jump me, watch me call them southside troops

And when that pistol in yo face, I bet yo bitch ass call it truce

Howard, Ion claim to be the best, but the better,

The Great Finesser, giving your ears as all the pleasure

The resurrector a great thinker and leader

No followers so fuck Tweeters, I speaker.

[Verse 2]

Shit they whip around in beakers, put over heaters

And pass out to all the geekers,

that's crack Motherfucker, I don't sell it, I spit it

Heard the flow one time, they'll be back in a minute,

I'm actually offended, Ian even notice a mention

It's how you present it, cadets lead yo fucking lieutenant

The sky's the limit, for those who ain't scared or timid

A damn shame, a damn shame, cause that's a small percentage

You must be dumb, deaf, or blind if you can't see the signs that
Howard are not a sequel,

We are but not equal, I talk to wise people, eat with wise men

Say steel sharp with steel, we'll let the filling begin

Staking on em' again, on my build and destroy

Hear momma yelling from heaven screaming, that's her boy

My hooks a backup Roy, Jones Jr. did you get it?

Pay attention it's imperative to listen

That's how ya stop pissing in the wind, like ya daddy say

I used to be a sleeping zombie, now I'm wide awake

If you can't read between the lines, you gon' fall for the bait

If you can't read between the lines, then you gon' fall for the bait.

[Hook]

Yeah, no surrender, no retreat I will never quit,

'till they put that fluid in me, and that death certificate

Give it to my closes kin, until then I'm going in

Yeah, until then I'm going in.

Margins of My Mind

(Connected to lyrics on next page)

I View "Mental Vacay" as a healthy habit sanctuary where *creativity* frees the mind. Through recording music, writing, and spoken words, we release the weight of stress and give our thoughts room to breathe. Let your intrusive thoughts flow freely, for in doing so, you reclaim control over your narrative. Remember, you have the power to shift your mindset and reshape your circumstances. Believe it. Receive it. Be it. Free your thoughts.

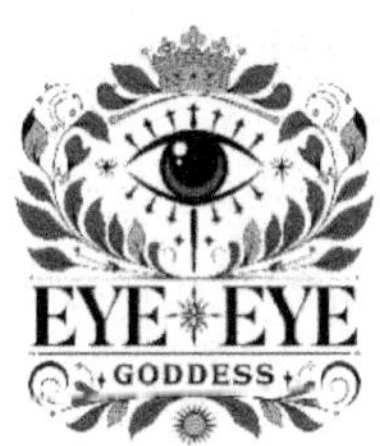

Mental Vacay

(Story Telling)

Intro

Yeah, yeah, yeah, yeah, hell yeah.

Yeah, yeah, yeah, hell yeah (hell yeah).

Let's go

[Verse 1]

Pain, stress, pressure. And if I had a bitch,

man, I probably wouldn't trust her.

No way, all day I smoke and drank to help me think

But nothing comes through.

And I don't like sunny days when the sky blue.

And I don't like a crowd so I should've bought a coupe.

That go vroom, and when you ask me for a ride I say it's no room
to get in

I stand out while y'all sit in, probably watching TV in ya mama den

I know it's fucked up race but you should get in,

they say not using yo talent is the biggest sin to me.

[Chorus]

(Repeat 2X)

I wish you could use my eyes to see,

What this fucked up world done to me.

[Hook]

I just need a mental vacation (echo) **(Repeat 4X)**

[Verse 2]

I close my eyes I'm in Hawaii,

Until I heard sirens flyin'-flyin'

Until I heard gunshots bangin'-bangin',

Until my telephone start rangin'-rangin',

I can't get a peace of mind, I can't get a peace of mind,

It's like the devil can read minds- can the devil read mine,

But why he gotta fuck with mine? -But why he gotta fuck with mine?

God knows it's been hard on our souls, cuts on our hands corns on our toes

Street with no lights, road with potholes,

Lil kid walkin' the street snot nose.

[Chorus]

(Repeat 4X)

It's all good, No it ain't (echo)

[Hook]

(Repeat 2X)

Vacation- what- I just need a mental vacation- what, what, what

Vacation- what- I just need a mental vacation- what, what, what

Survival of the Fittest

(S.O.F)

[Hook]

(Repeat 2X)

We gon' ride till we get it

Tell me if you with it

One life to live, we livin'

Steady chasing them digits,

It's survival of the fittest babe

It's survival of the fittest.

[Verse 1]

Cow eats the grass, and the man eats the cow,

The King is at the table, take a bow before you chow.

It's both cutthroat and foul, never throw in the towel,

Don't argue with a fool and keep it wiser than an owl.

The beasts are on the prowl, looking for their prey,

Fight or flight, kicks in, so you see another day.

So, save that bouquet, the funeral here soon,

I'm more wolf than a sheep, bitch I'm howling at the moon (echo).

Yeah, we bend but we don't break,

We come first and we leave late,

We go in, no hesitate, just to make sure we get straight.

It's no escape from the lion's den,

Once yo ass step in, then -yo ass in (yo ass in).

End of story, nigga, closed case,

And it's hard as hell for them to solve a- cold case (cold case),

It's survival, it's a tough task,

If y'n ain't built Ford tough,

Then -you won't last (you won't last).

Margins of My Mind

(Connected to lyrics on next page)

75

This flow of brilliance asks a single

question, what is the point?
Meaning lives within our influence, in our intentions, and in the
company we keep.
if no true purpose anchors what we create or who we are
becoming?

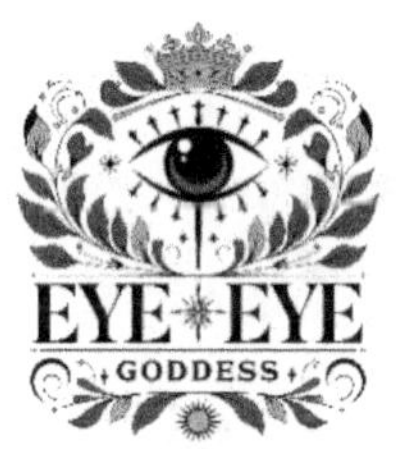

What's The Point?

[Intro]

(Repeat 3X)

What's the point, What's the score?

[Verse]

What's the point? Is we really taking score?

Is a rich man's life worth more than a poor?

Do I give you a bore because I speak my mind?

Or would you rather live your life blissfully blind?

Is it a crime to think outside the box?

Hair like wool, I bet Jesus had locs.

Ciroc on the rocks, make you feel on top.

But when you get pulled over, it's a DUI drop.

Shit, I doubt it. If you're bout it, read a book.

Tell 'em, prove it while you look.

Then throw that shit back at 'em.

Baby, this is what it took.

What it took for a fact to be a fact.

And just because I'm Black, they think knowledge I lack.

What's the point? What's the point just to stunt like my daddy?

Working two jobs just to buy that new caddy.

Them hoes going crazy, but them hoes been batty.

'Cause they never wanted love, they just wanted sugar daddies.

As-salamu alaykum, make a nigga feel good.

But pork the only meat we can afford in the hood.

The boys in the hood hate they born in the hood,

But the boys in the burbs wish they born in the hood.

What's the point? What's the point?

'Cause them niggas never listen.

I bet smartest nigga probably dead or in prison.

Or standing on the stage 'cause a bullet missed his head.

If I don't tell the truth, I would be better off dead.

What's the point?

Bottom-out

[Verse]

Wish they would've told me I was born in the trap - trap.

Ma was on that butter back and forth, she relapses - relapse.

Pa was on it too, but a functioning addict- addict

Guess you ain't no addict-addict if you control your habits.

What's sad is a slim chance for a nigga like me.

Thank God right now, I ain't dead in these streets.

Thank 'em for these beats, it help my soul bleed,

coming from the bottom, I ain't got no one but me, but who, but me, but who

Trust drugs, money, sex, my best friend and company,

dark days turn sunny when I hit the weed.

I get on the mic, I make my soul bleed.

They say it comes from greed, but I just want my piece of the pie.

I be fucked up, so I look to the sky.

I know I'm on the clock, so Ima grind 'til I die.

So I, tighten up and give my mercy to the man above.

'Cause this his land before I go, I wash my hands.

Gone.

My Heart Between His Lines

(Connected to lyrics on next page)

The ongoing struggle in America, particularly seen through the lens of police brutality, reflects a long history of systemic injustice. The belief that race justifies oppression continues to divide and shape power dynamics. Being seen as a threat simply because of one's appearance is a painful reality.

But your skin should never define your worth or divide your humanity. What both B. Howard (Howard Soul) and EyeNEye Goddess want most is for you to feel proud of who you are. You matter. You deserve to smile. Embracing self-pride honors your identity. Through art and music, we find strength, healing, and connection — reminding us that we're not alone. Look into your soul and be proud of yourself.

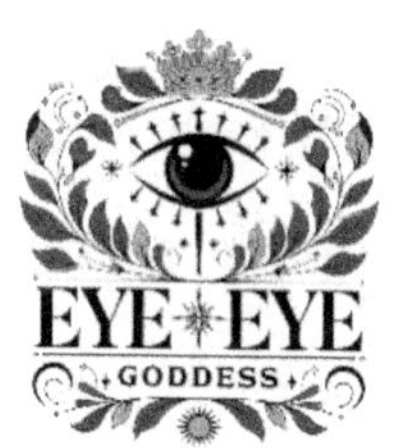

Black Lives Matter

(BLM)

[Intro]

Okay, Please don't shoot, please don't shoot me (It's like my little tribute to Black Lives, you know Black Lives do matter) Please don't shoot, please don't shoot me, me, Please don't shoot, please don't shoot me, me yeah, yeah Please don't shoot, please don't shoot me, me Yeah and I say, please don't shoot, please don't shoot me, Ima, fill all that in later...

[Verse 1]

And I say, please don't shoot, 'cause my skin got melanin.

Say monkey, our closest kin.

But I disagree again, Mr. Cracker of the whip, captain of the ship.

I'm a field nigga at heart, but I keep waves and a temp, just to fit in they society.

Scared when you got dreads, so they feel safe to hide me.

But I'm for black propriety, KKK my rivalry, so full of shit.

How you claim to be a Christian, but racist as shit?

Put a bag over your head, burning crosses in the lawn.

Snatch that bag off your hand, and you can see that you a pawn,

On a grand scale.

Had Indians, for niggas off in tobacco fields.

But they got sick as hell, they left they own country.

'Cause they couldn't play by the rules,

They made their own country. Where they can make all the rules,

They say I'm so country. But I know what I know (I know), this land was made for white men to prosper and grow.

[Hook]

And I say, please don't shoot, please don't shoot me

Please don't shoot, please don't shoot me, me, me

Please don't shoot, yeah please don't shoot me, me-me-me

Please don't shoot, shoot please don't shoot me, me, me

Please don't shoot, please don't shoot me, me, me

[Verse 2]

I'm a young Black male, all my partners in jail.

All my role models in prison, so I ain't got time to listen.

To the land of free, home of brave.

It's 2015, I'm still feeling like a slave.

And on my grave, let it say where a real nigga lay.

'Til the angels blow they horn, and I meet up with Ethel Mae.

So pay me some attention, like a baby in the kitchen.

Around knives and fire, I keep rounds to fire.

As of oppressors and molesters, I can't raise kids.

How you tell a three-year-old being Black ain't fair?

I should tell my niece she's born handicapped,

With the color of her skin, and the color of her hair – hair.

So please don't shoot.

[Hook]

Please don't shoot, please don't shoot me yeah, yeah, yeah

Please don't shoot, please don't shoot me, me, me

Please don't shoot, yeah please don't shoot me, me-me-me

Please don't shoot, shoot please don't shoot me, me, me

Please don't shoot, please don't shoot me, me, me

Artifact

Rare pictures of Howard Soul and EyeNEye Goddess at an in-house studio. These highlights were captured during a memorable era after *Moonshine Music*—recorded in those raw, late-night "Moonshine hours" where Howard Soul was born. We were straight shot out, as usual, locked in: he focused on the computer shaping the beat, and I zoned in on the hook, ready to bring the heat. #LockedIn #AfterHours

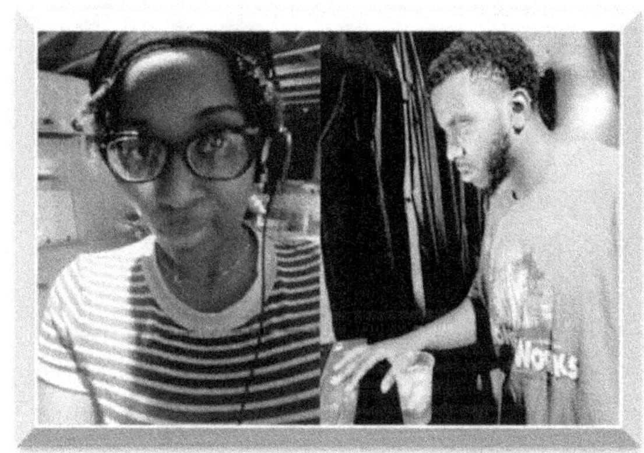

"Fall 2018 — different angles. Howard Soul, and I in the lab, crafting a duo. No sleep—just laughter, vibes, and raw creation"

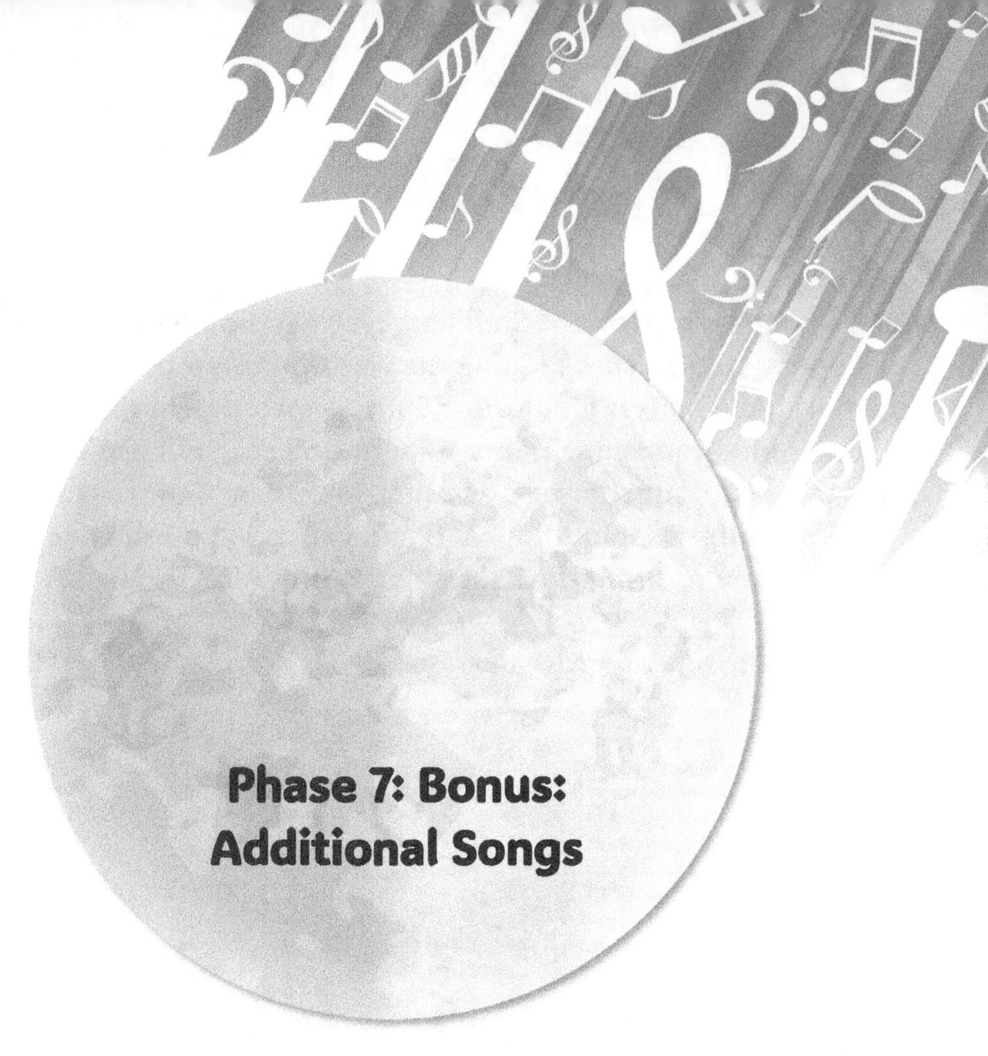
Phase 7: Bonus:
Additional Songs

Eternal Resonance

(Connected to lyrics on next page)

"Bobsleighed" was crafted in 2015. It has a perfect fusion of *creativity, culture, and cognizance,* embodying the dual artistry of B. Howard (Howard Soul). The track delivers a calm yet high-energy vibe, highlighting versatility in both sound and spirit. With rich expression and emotional resonance, it takes you on an introspective journey. To me, this message serves as a reminder to stay grounded — cause VET sit low like a bobsleighed. This will always be a classic song, carrying a lot of personal meaning.

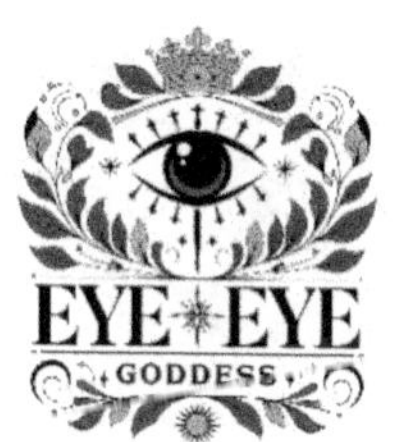

Bobsleighed

[Intro]

Bobsleighed, I always wanted a VET, that shit that MF
So sexy, you know how low that shit sit, sit so MF sexy.
bobsleighed.

[Hook]

(Repeat 2X)

Bobsleighed, VET sit low like you bobsleighed,
Two straps, nigga, you ain't gon' rob nothin',
Better whoasah home, don't start nothin'
I got a lot to lose, but I'll lose it all for nothin',
Bobsleighed.

[Verse]

People all around me, rushin' like Jadeveon Clowney.
The quicker picker upper, she suck me up like bounty.
My partner had two weed brownies, I ate 'em and got geeked,
My cup had two Xans, I popped 'em and fell asleep.
I think that was last week, my memory fading out.
Got a show in South Carolina, tomorrow we heading out.
Heard there 5 percenters there, know they'll hear me loud and clear.

As we build and born the youth, probably die for spitting the truth,

And that don't stop me.

Look how they did Gaddafi, Malcolm, King, or any nigga with a dream.

I bring a dealer team when I'm in the booth,

Running circles 'round these rappers, singing duck, duck, goose.

[Hook]

(Repeat 8x)

VET sit low

[Hook]

Bobsleighed, VET sit low like ya bobsleighed,

Two straps, nigga, you ain't gone rob nothin',

Better whoasah home, don't start nothin'

I got a lot to lose, but I'll lose it all for nothin',

Bobsleighed.

[Verse 2]

Fuck the barbershop talk, LeBron and the Cavs,

Regardless of your team, I'm still gon' need half to add up, to wholes, mo preferably elbows.

Been stuck in the hell hole so long that it feels cold to me.

I talk to the Devil the other day, he said Howard, what it do?

You should of chose another way, and he right.

I feel like I'm stuck off in a matrix, like I could change the world but I'll die trying to save it.

Fast cars, fast broads is overrated, bitches getting booty shots to feel more a lady, shit' crazy.

Hard to do work unless shit pays, but how the fuck I'm gonna survive off of minimum wage?

And why the fuck should I trust the folks who made us slaves?

Like I believe in God but Ion know who wrote that page, the Bible, liable to be some shit made up.

Say who the chosen people is, they could of switched that up.

They saying, Howard, you chill before they shut you up.

I gotta die one day and I don't give two fucks.

They saying Howard, you chill before they shut you up,

I got to die one day and I don't give two fucks, let's go.

[Spoken Outro]

And so, what I be trying to do is, I be wanting shit to ride, but I be trying to say some real shit, really rapping but it be some more shit I be trying to teach at the same time, real shit...iight.

Blow

[Intro]

Yeah, yeah, yeah, I can hear myself good.

Yeah, yeah, yeah

Let me ask these niggas something huh.

[Hook]

How much can you take before you break, my nigga? - How much can you take?

How much can you take before you fold? - for you fold.

Do you know yo limit? Do you know yo limit? - Do you know yo limit?

How much can you take before you blow? - fore you blow.

Cause it's pressure - cause its pressure.

[Post Hook]

When you're out here (when you out here)

Ain't no locksmith (ain't no locksmith)

Got the keys (got the keys)

So it's best to (so it's best to)

Keep your head up (keep your head up)

When you out here (when you out here)

In these streets (in these streets).

[Verse]

A whole lot can happen in a little bit of time.

Real nigga shit, I'm tired of coloring in the lines.

Real nigga shit, I'm bout to rob a nigga blind.

Cause real nigga shit, I feel I'm running out of time.

It's 60 seconds in a minute, shit can change in a minute.

I had talked to bruh Thursday, and by Friday he was finished.

Off-The-Cuff

(Freestyle)

I told my lil' bruh I'm in this world but I'm not of it.

Accept my consequences as they come, then rise above it.

Cause when you born Black, being good won't cut it.

Say if you born Black, being good won't cut it.

Supreme being, 5 percenter, I don't make excuses.

I use wisdom to untie me from they nooses and break they chain.

Yeah, I'm reminded it's a God every time it rains.

They say you got to break a buck just to get some change.

They say to get the best cut, you go against the grain.

A seasoned vet pays attention to the finer things.

My eyes open wide, heart full with pride.

Ancestor blood in my veins, so they still alive.

For real, I make the Bible come true, Ima stick to the script till I'm richer than a Jew.

They say my flow cold but it's sicker than the flu,

And what's the use of having wings if you're living in the zoo?

Okay, so I ain't holding shit back,

Hope you get hit by a train, cause you keep lying on the track.

A hoe is just a bitch who make her money on her back,

And I work better when my back against the wall like a tack.

I told my homeboy, Karama do matter.

He said, "Fuck you, pay me," to a nigga, hang a cracker.

He said, "Fuck you, pay me," till they find a cure for cancer.

Then said, "Fuck you, pay me," Brian Karama don't matter.

I say, well that's what works for me.

Every time I'm in the dark, I get enough light to see.

Every time my stomach growls, I get enough food to eat.

And if I need a little more, then I just cut another beat, I swear.

News

[Hook]

(Repeat 14X)

Y'n heard the news

[Verse 1]

You ain't heard the news? Get your head out your anus.

I been stayin' down, now I'm close to rich and famous.

I step on the stage, and proceed to go brainless.

Popped two Lortab, now a nigga feeling painless.

Yup, yup, numb to the world, hard to make me smile,

Hard to make me cry. Hardbody nigga,

Girl, I'm that guy. Aye, fuck that nigga, girl,

I'm that guy. Now, extra, extra, read all about it.

I keep it club crowded, and I'm country like howdy.

Yes sir, yes sir, yee haw, yee haw.

You ain't heard, like sushi I'm raw.

Nigga up and coming by far. This much away from star.

If I said it I meant it, that's law.

I used to keep that thang in the car.

Now I keep that thang in my draws.

When niggas be poppin' at the mouth,

And really want to take me out.

But either way I'm straight.

9 outta 10 that shit won't escape.

Nigga can't take food off my plate.

If he do, that's my mistake.

But I'll just catch his ass later with the K.

Reel his ass in, get his ass with the bait.

Not too early, not too late.

If you don't hear the news?

You'll see the yellow tape, I swear.

[Hook]

(Repeat 14X)

Y'n heard the news

[Verse 2]

You think you better than Howard?

You must be fucking with me.

Boy, they call me abstinence cause ain't nobody fucking with me.

Hope you ain't fucking with me. Got that little oven with me.

Bake or broil whatever nigga, it's nothing to me.

That's the killer swag for yo monkey ass.

This is swag ed, I hope you ain't been skipping class.

Got that hippie swag I'm forever twisting grass.

And got that rebel in me. All y'all can kiss my ass.

No! bet you can't do it like me, you lil copycat.

Because my style's original, and you can copy that.

Plus, you's a sloppy cat. Laughed at in yo habitat.

Little nigga, 5 foot 7 but I ain't having that.

Tell 'em what happened, last time I ripped the track.

Owner of the studio said he ain't even want me back.

Cause that boy burned down yo roof.

Y'n heard, I'm more realer than the truth, so stop playin', hoe.

[Hook]

(Repeat 14X)

Y'n heard the news

[Verse 3]

Now, you can catch me at the studio on Icehouse.

But before the night's out, I might be in yo wife's mouth.

Now that's a low blow. Midget with a flute.

If you a worker, not a boss, then I suggest you follow suit, nigga.

Club's lit, blood shed all over the beat.

Cause I killed the motherfucker, spittin' nothing but that heat.

You look tired and expired. I suggest you take a seat.

Bout to run it on yo corner like the coach just called a sweep.

Right now, fuck that rapping beat.

Cause y'all use to that three feet.

Meaning all that shit be weak.

They can't swim, no compete splash.

Free my boy, Bantana, and my playa, Panta, Chris.

Bull Dog too, and all the hustlers behind the fence.

Screamin' power to the people, motherfuck Willie Lynch.

If you scared, say you scared, then sit yo ass on the bench.

Touchdown in yo city like I had a QB with me.

I didn't have nobody with me, but I made yo team look shitty damn.

[Hook]

(Repeat 14X)

Y'n heard the news

Stick and Move

(Freestyle)

Born a bastard boy by definition

Runnin' in Grandma's kitchen

Made me go and pull my switches

Too big for my britches she would say when I misbehave

Now I'm putting flowers on her grave

Damn I miss them days.

Growing up, knew I would be rich fore I was 21

Seeing dope boys with nice cars, Ima get me one, never happen

Still rappin' that real shit, 38 my kill switch

Saving up for that F and N

Praising Jah on the West end, Shalom my G,

I come in peace, Niggas on that monkey see, Monkey do,

can't fuck with you. Teach you how to stick and move

Cautious when I'm walking through, 'cause I don't like the vibe of
you

And yo partner shaky too, on my square like Masons do

Reppin' for fame, I never want that

I popped the wrong pill and Ian never come back

I see spirits, I see demon's, Ion see people, I see souls,

On these beats I rock and roll, Keep it lit like burning coal

Margins of My Mind

(Connected to lyrics on next page)

"Cutthroat" is one of those tracks where B. Howard shines. His flow stands out, showcasing his lyrical skill. He balances *creativity* with cultural insight, exploring the impact of personal choices. The vivid imagery and edgy, catchy hook make it resonate deeply.

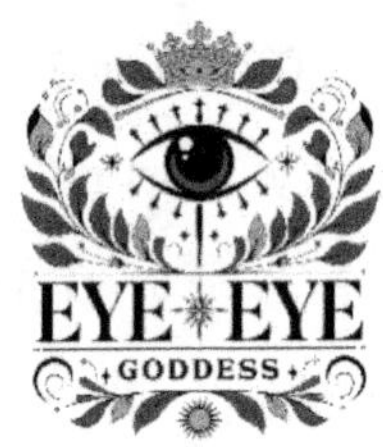

Cut-throat

[Hook]

Cut, Throat (Repeat 4X)

This world is full of lies and thieves,

This world is full of lust and greed.

[Verse 1]

I'm getting' older, no mo lean

Getting' older, no mo bean,

I don't even want no molly,

Even though they call 'em clean

The piff I'm with hollering

Bitch, I'm with called Power Spring

Cause her nose keep powdering, every time she round the scene

Or a mirror on a wall

Broke so long I got to ball

But don't quote me on this at all

Cause I might start right back tomorrow

Relapsing like addicts do. Now everybody mad at you

But we do what we have to do.

When we low on capital, At Atlanta the capital

Where the weight man throw a pack at chu

Tell you go get tactical. And don't talk when they have to.

Or that head a get bust to the white meat

Yellow tape a lot of blood on the streets.

Cut, Throat (Repeat 4X)

This world is full of lies and thieves,

This world is full of lust and greed.

[Verse 2]

They let 'em go from the Eagles like they name was McNeab,

And I ain't talking bout no ribs when I say cutting them slabs

Stop playing monopoly when I say I'm on the ave

This craft is straight cheese, but you can't put it in yo grits-nope

Early in the morning, this how they feed the bricks

From zone one to six, roc roller and pit.

The bomb and bricks is right next to the stick

But when 12 come.

Hope yo young ass can jump a fence

No there's no mercy for the weak here, weak here

Fuck around, get sat down till next leap year

And that's at least four years if you think about it

But that's why y'on like my flow, you gotta think about it

So think about it.

[Hook]

Cut, Throat (Repeat 4X)

This world is full of lies and thieves,

This world is full of lust and greed.

The Last Verse

They say to keep your soul alive, you must sing. Eye believe that to stay aligned, you must also dream. In these dreams, we uncover identity, find the courage to heal, carry legacy, and awaken purpose— restoring balance to life. Together, we amplify the beauty of this world through pure love, healing laughter, and truth spoken freely. Each voice holds its own rhythm, and when shared with intention, becomes connection—within and between us. Love teaches us slowly through kindness and through patience. There is no single path to reach it. Understanding often comes later, after love has already changed us. Your songs and dreams will rise, echoing a healing rhythm within the soul, reminding us that who we are and who we become is shaped by how deeply we love. Here's to unconditional love, Brian.

Eye carry you with me in everything Eye do— for you, for myself, and for the people.

— EyenEye Goddess

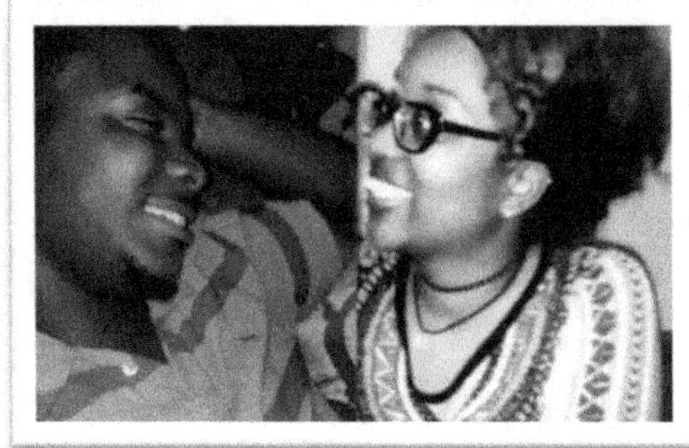

"Same year, 2014 different moments — two souls caught in a gaze"

Phase 8: A Journey of Purpose, Gratitude, and Legacy

From the earliest stages of building this vision to navigating the unique layers that shaped its voice, I am both proud and humbled. It is a privilege to uphold Brian's legacy through the creative duality of B. Howard (Howard Soul). Together, we tapped into lyrics, *creativity, culture, and cognizance*, and experiences with memories — creating something rooted in authenticity. In shaping this lyrical memoir, I have put together personal reflections, journaled moments, and autobiographical insights to honor some of our shared times and the journey still unfolding—rooted in identity, healing, legacy, purpose, and love. This path has been richly creative, and I give thanks to the Most High for the gift of walking it.

Let this work stand as a reminder to cultivate *creativity, culture, and cognizance* in your daily life. Communication is more than expression—it is a tool for healing, understanding, and transformation. Use it to uplift, connect, and spark meaningful change. In moments of chaos or uncertainty, pause. Breathe. Release what you cannot control. Reflect on what you can. Then move forward with intention. Never doubt the power of your voice or the value of your story. Love yourself deeply, trust your process, and honor the gifts you carry. You are enough, always have been, always will be. This journey of purpose, gratitude, and legacy is yours to shape, and it matters.

Thank You

Thank you for being part of this journey and for taking the time to offer your support. I'm especially grateful to those who stood by me, offering your heart, hands, and mind in encouragement, sharing thoughtful insights, and providing honest critique along the way. You know who you are and the role you played in shaping this work. Your dedication, communication, and willingness to show up made all the difference. I hold that with deep gratitude.

Final Word

I trust that the birth of this experience will echo and inspire hearts and minds — rooting us in the rich intersection of art, literature, and beyond that shapes our stories and uplifts our communities. ***Celebrating Moonshine Music: Creativity, Culture, & Cognizance*** is more than a title; it's a tribute to the *culture*. The vision is to become a sacred space where aspiring writers speak their truths,

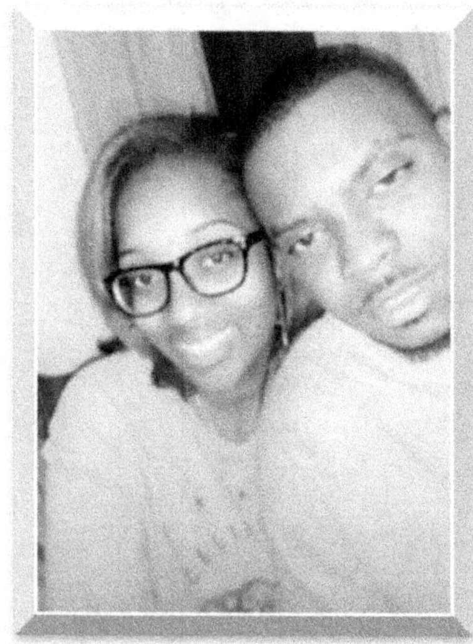

honor the voices that came before and beyond, and carry the legacy forward through the power of creative expression and everyday experiences. This isn't just an ending, it's a rising. Remain steadfast in your dreams, hold your vision steady, and let your truth guide you upward. May peace ground you, purpose guide you, and good energy light your path. Hold it down, Forward progress always. Peace and blessings.

"On a sacred day of remembrance in 2016, your presence was so grounded, heartfelt, and deeply appreciated, I really needed the support

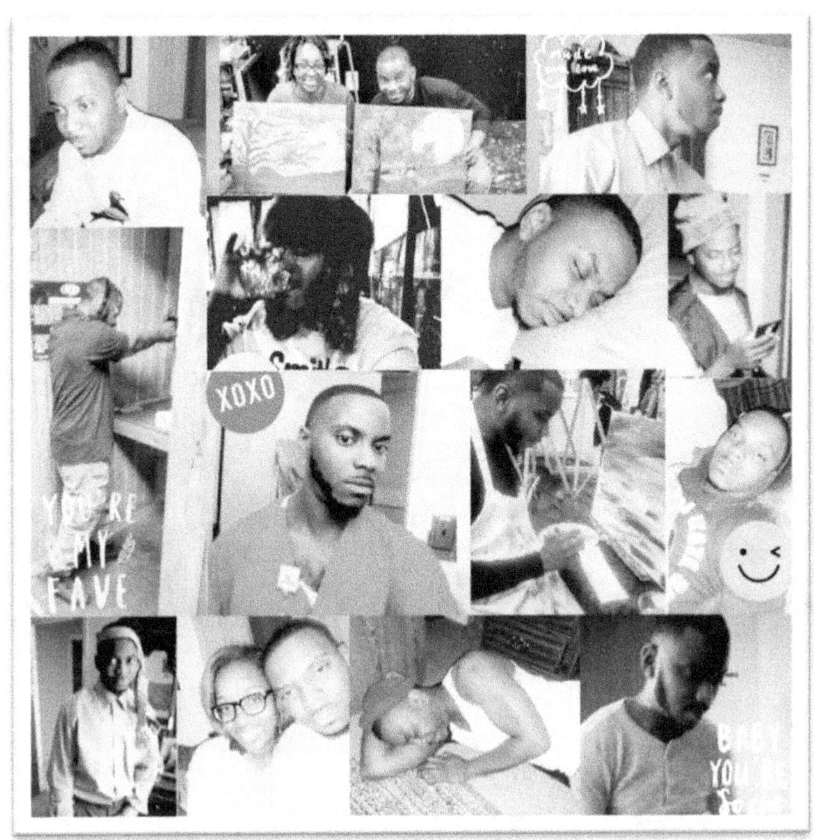

"A collage of moments — Brian, B. Howard (Howard Soul) legacy — capturing some of the many energies, emotions, and random highlights of his journey. I appear here too, holding space in memory. This page stands as a reflection before the final tribute, where one image carries the weight of farewell"

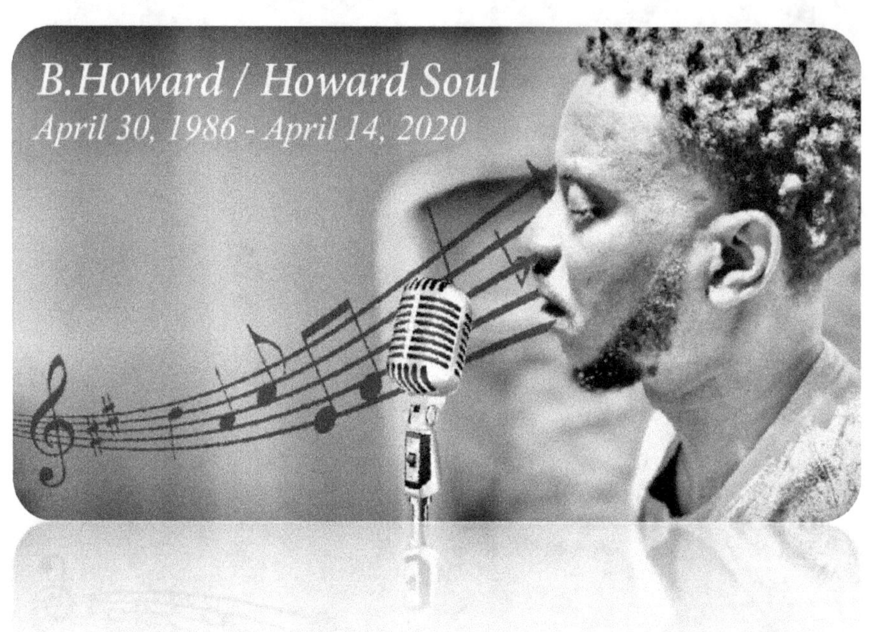

To the life, spirit, and legacy of B. Howard (Howard Soul).
You are honored, fully and deeply. What we shared lives on — not as sorrow, but as fuel. I carry the best of you with me in every step, every song, every moment of purpose. Your presence has shaped my journey, vision, and the path ahead, echoing the essence of your life and the blessings the Creator poured into me through you. Forever grateful for your gift, you have left an indelible imprint on my soul, inspiring me to carry it forward to do the same in my own way. Long Live B. Howard (Howard Soul).

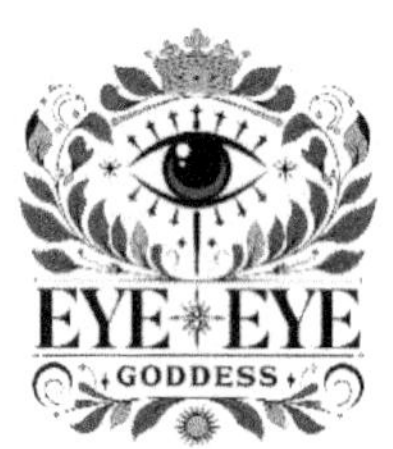

www.ingramcontent.com/pod-product-compliance
Lightning Source LLC
Chambersburg PA
CBHW061321120726
48001CB00002B/616

DEDICATION

This book is dedicated to every single person who has been hurt, confused, or disappointed while dating. To those who have tried to do it the world's way and ended up broken, tired, or lost—this is for you. To the women and men who are tired of going in circles, who feel like they've been following all the rules but still come up empty, and to those who have compromised along the way and now wonder if they can ever get back on track: **there's hope for you.**

This book is also dedicated to the ones who have held onto their faith and purity despite the pressure of the culture. I honor you for standing ten toes down on waiting on God, and for not giving in. Whether you've been walking faithfully or you've made mistakes along the way, God's grace is more than enough to meet you where you are.

Lastly, to my husband and children—this is for you. Your love and support have shown me what it means to live a life that honors God in everything, including relationships. I am forever grateful for our beautiful love story!